Executive Coaching:

A Perception of the Chief Executive Officers of the Most Successful Fortune 500 Companies

by

Sam Fanasheh

ISBN: 1-58112- 286-1

DISSERTATION.COM

Boca Raton, Florida
USA • 2005

Executive Coaching: A Perception of the Chief Executive Officers of the Most Successful Fortune 500 Companies

Copyright © 2003 Sam Fanasheh

Dissertation.com
Boca Raton, Florida
USA • 2005

ISBN: 1-58112- 286-1

The Perception of Executive Coaching Among CEOs of America's Top 500 Companies

A Dissertation Presented to

The Faculty of the Graduate School of Education and Psychology

Pepperdine University

_____

In Partial Fulfillment of the Requirements for the Degree

Doctor of Education in Organizational Leadership

_____

By

Husam A. Fanasheh

March, 2003

This dissertation, written by

Husam Abdalla Fanasheh

under the guidance of a Faculty Committee and approved by its members, has been submitted to and accepted by the Graduate Faculty in partial fulfillment of the requirements for the degree of

DOCTOR OF EDUCATION

Date: December 9, 2002

Faculty Committee

_____
June Schmieder-Ramirez, Ph.D., Chairperson

_____
Lois Blackmore, Ed.D.

_____
Ram C. Madan, Ph.D.

                              _____
                              Robert C. Paull, Ph.D.
                              Associate Dean

                              _____
                              Margaret J. Weber, Ph.D.
                              Dean

TABLE OF CONTENTS

LIST OF TABLES

LIST OF FIGURES

ACKNOWLEDGMENTS

Many people played vital roles in the preparation of this dissertation. Some helped with financial support, others gave me personal inspiration, and still others provided much needed information and assistance. I am so grateful to those people, and in particular: Dr. June Schmieder-Ramirez, dissertation committee chair; Mr. Bob Souza, The Boeing Company, personal coach; The Learning Together Program, The Boeing Company, financial assistance; Alison Carter, Institute of Employment Studies, England, literature; and above all, his mighty "AllA" for his support and inspiration.

I am also grateful to my wife, Dr. Rania Tamimi, for her continuous support and those beautiful meals she prepared as I typed, and the little miracle that she produced during this project named Meera.

Finally, this dissertation is dedicated to my mother Khadra Mousa, and my father Abdalla Fanasheh. May "AllA" bless them.

<u>VITA</u>

EXPERIENCE

1998-Present:	Production Manager, C-17 Aircraft, The Boeing Company.
1996-1998	The Boeing Company: Quality Engineering, C17 Program.
1995-1996	JDA Associates, Airport Modeler (TAAM Software).
1994-1995	USAir : Crystal City, VA. Strategic Planner and Market Analyst.
1993-1994	ERAU : Daytona Beach, FL. FAA licensed repair station, Reciprocating Engines Overhaul.
1991-1993	NCATO : Cairo, Egypt, Airframe & Powerplant, Cessna-172.
1989-1991	Egypt Air : Cairo, Egypt, B737 Airframe & Powerplant .
1988-1989	Anderson Consulting: Cairo, Egypt.
1987-1987	Tourism, Marriott: Cairo, Egypt.

HONORS

- Silver Eagle, The Boeing Company, 2000.
- Employee of The Month, Aug. 1998, A&T, The Boeing Company.
- Three Dale Carnegie Leadership Awards, 1999-2000.
- Lead Man Award (Cairo Airport), NCATO s Leadership Award, Delta Mu Delta Honor Society, Who s Who in American Universities and Colleges 1995/96, Dean s List, and Honor Roll.
- Member of the American Association of Airport Executives (AAAE).

- Member of Boeing s Leadership Development Program, Long Beach, CA.

EDUCATION

- **Master of Business Administration: Embry Riddle Aeronautical University, Daytona Beach, Florida, 1997**
- Bachelor of Science in Aviation Maintenance Management: Embry Riddle Aeronautical University, Daytona Beach, Florida, 1994
- Associate of Science in Aviation Maintenance Technology: NCATO/Cairo, Egypt, 1992
- Project Management: University of California at Irvine, 1998.

ABSTRACT OF THE DISSERTATION

THE PERCEPTION OF EXECUTIVE COACHING
AMONG CEOs OF AMERICA'S TOP 500 COMPANIES

BY
HUSAM ABDALLA FANASHEH

DOCTOR OF EDUCATION IN ORGANIZATIONAL LEADERSHIP

THE GRADUATE SCHOOL OF EDUCATION AND PSYCHOLOGY

PEPPERDINE UNIVERSITY, 2002

DR. JUNE SCHMIEDER-RAMIREZ, CHAIRPERSON

The study explored the perception of executive coaching
among the chief executive officers (CEOs) of America's
largest 500 companies as shown on *Fortune* magazine list of
April 15, 2002.

This study utilized an instrument of 12 questions. The
questionnaire was sent to the CEOs of the top 500 American
companies. A cover letter and a self-addressed, postage-paid
envelope were provided. Attribute responses were coded and
analyzed using several descriptive statistical tools.

Out of the 500 targeted CEOs, 143 participated in this
study. Seventy-six percent of the respondents demonstrated a
good understanding of the basic concepts of executive
coaching. Eighty-three percent were able to distinguish
coaching from consulting, 61% stated that coaching can make
their life somewhat better, 49% agreed on the idea of hiring

executive coaches, and 32% declared that they had hired coaches.

Those who never hired a coach showed a great deal of willingness (37%) to hire one. Sixty-two percent of the respondents indicated a preference for coaches from outside their organizations, 51% would search for one through human resources, 31% preferred sites off their company premises for coaching sessions, and 43% would keep their coaching relationship confidential.

Thirty-nine percent of the participants expressed the belief that coaching should not be limited to a specific management level, and 37% said they supported research related to executive coaching.

Based on these findings, executive coaching can be considered as a worthwhile investment. Future studies may take a closer look at the details and characteristics of the coaching session, and may explore what is called the "trusted advisor," someone who is believed to be much closer to the client than is the coach.

Chapter 1

Introduction

The collapse of Enron Corporation and the mysterious conduct of its accounting consultant, Arthur Anderson, are strong indications that leadership is no longer simply a matter of technical and business knowledge. Rather, leadership is more about interpersonal relationships and the political skills that are crucial for the survival of the organization in today's competitive business environment.

Bianco and Lavelle (2000) reported that in today s fierce environments, chief executive officers become victims as a result of technological change and poor execution. Even the best CEOs drop like flies due to enormous expectations, impatient investors, slowing economy and the little time they were allowed to prove themselves (p. 86). In recent years (Figure 1), the mounting turnover at the top has taken on the aspect of a crisis as one CEO after another has been given the boot or forced to resign (Bianco & Lavelle, 2000).

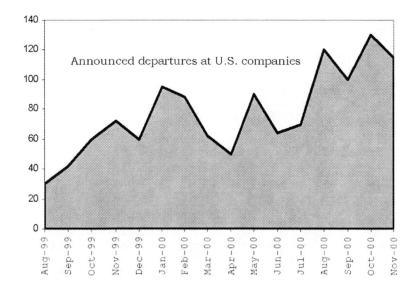

Figure 1. CEO turnover.
Note. From The CEO Trap, by A. Bianco and L. Lavelle, 2000,
BusinessWeek. Copyright 2000 by A. Bianco and L. Lavelle.
Reprinted with permission.

To reverse this trend, more and more executives from
the United States and Great Britain are opening their doors
to executive coaches. Literature from the United Kingdom
indicates a strong and positive perception of executive
coaching among English executives. Surveys carried out in
the Kingdom indicated that many English executives not only
believe in executive coaching but also spend somewhere
around 15% of their salary on coaches (Carter, 2001).

The objective of this study was to take a closer look
at the perception of this service among the chief executive
officers of America's top 500 companies, those companies
ranked by *Fortune 500* according to their annual revenue. The

study not only defines the executive's perception of this service in the United States but also gives coaches a clearer idea of the strategies and styles most clients prefer. The study was inspired through research carried out by the Institute of Employment Studies in Great Britain which produced a wealth of knowledge about executive coaching in the new millennium.

Problem statement

The high rate of turnover among American CEOs creates out of executive coaching, from the coaches' view, a viable tool. Yet a broad question persists: what level of help, considering the turnover rate, can executive coaching offer?

Research Questions

The study responds to the following questions:

1.1 What proportion of CEOs of America's top 500 companies are aware of executive coaching services?

1.2 Of CEOs who are aware of executive coaching, what proportion are able to distinguish coaching from consulting?

1.3 What proportion of CEOs believe in the benefits of executive coaching?

1.4 What proportion of CEOs are willing to hire an executive coach?

1.5 When hiring a coach, do CEOs prefer coaches from outside their organization?

1.6 What proportion of CEOs prefer to keep the entire coaching process confidential?

1.7 What channels do CEOs use to hire coaches?

1.8 What proportion of CEOs believe that executive coaching should be limited to a particular management level?

1.9 What proportion of CEOs have preferences as to location where coaching sessions should be conducted (at company headquarters or somewhere else)?

1.10 What proportion of CEOs support research for executive coaching?

Purpose of The Study

The purpose of this study was to identify the perception of executive coaching among chief executive officers of America's top 500 companies. The study targeted the extent to which executives are willing to deal with executive coaches and which approaches to coaching they would be most likely to accept.

The study assessed the following:

- CEOs understanding of the term *executive coaching*.

- CEOs exposure to studies of executive coaching.

- Whether CEOs believe in the benefits of executive coaching.

- CEOs attitude toward hiring an executive coach.

- What settings CEOs preferred for coaching sessions.

- What level of support CEOs would provide for executive coaching.

- Whether coaching should be limited to a particular executive level.

Importance of The Study

The outcome of this study set forth how executive coaching is viewed among CEOs of the top 500 companies in the United States as of Summer 2002. The study also lays a solid foundation for those who choose coaching for their career. In addition, it introduces coaching to the general public as a professional service, one that can be clearly distinguished from consulting. Armed with the information and insights gathered by this study, executives and executive coaches should be able to put their new knowledge to work and to increase the profitability of their companies.

Limitations of The Study

The study was limited in the following ways:

- The study was conducted among United States-based businesses (Appendix A) and does not reflect the international opinion of executive coaching.

- Since CEOs resist spending the time to answer open-ended questionnaires, the study utilized a closed-end questionnaire (Appendix B).

Assumptions

The following assumptions were central in this study:

- The CEOs themselves, not someone else from their office, responded to the questionnaire.

- The respondents gave valid responses to all sections of the questionnaire.

Definition of Terms

Executive Coaching

Stefanie Pryor (1994) of the Boston University School of Management defined *executive coaching* as:

> A process in which a coach and a client work together in targeting a personal and/or career effectiveness need or opportunity and setting concrete goals to improve the behavior in a limited period of time through open questioning, private feedback, and exposure of one s self esteem, i.e. personal vulnerability. (p. 2)

Perception

According to the Webster s New World Dictionary, *perception* can be defined as the awareness, knowledge and belief of a certain concept.

Chief Executive Officer

The title *Chief Executive Officer*, or *CEO*, is often interchangeable with *president*. The term *CEO* is widely accepted for describing the head of the executives; internationally the president or CEO is often called *managing director* (Benton, 1996).

Fortune 500

Headquartered in New York, the Fortune500 magazine is not only ... the ultimate measure of American business; it's also the story of American business, one year at a time . Criteria for membership in this elite club [remains] constant: revenues, revenues, revenues (*Fortune*, 2002, p. 1).

Chapter 2

Literature Review

Introduction

Ellen Stuhlmann of the *Executive Insider* newsletter, claimed that "four out of ten executives fail within the first 18 months in their new positions" (2000, p. 2). A year earlier, Charan and Colvin, in an attempt to explain the causes of such failures, stated, "it s rarely for lack of smarts or vision. Most unsuccessful CEOs stumble because of one simple, fatal shortcoming" (1999, p. 68). And while many executives prefer to work this issue out on their own, few call on executive coaches for help. This chapter defines executive coaching, examines the need for it, and identifies the process of executive coaching.

The complexity of today s business environment, on the one hand, and the pressures executives may be experiencing in their lives, on the other, often cause them to develop fatal blind spots. Such blind spots, if not detected early and remedied immediately, could lead to the ruin of both their business and their life. The impaired vision of their CEOs drove two-thirds of all major companies worldwide to replace their CEO at least once since 1995, and more than 1,000 United States CEOs have left office over the past 12 months alone (Bianco & Lavelle, 2000, p. 86).

Although chief executive officers tend to be dedicated, intelligent, and articulate, they still have a need for honest feedback to which they must adapt (Dastrala & McLarney, 2001). Executive coaching is probably one of the most powerful techniques of feedback simply because a coach, in contrast to any other staff member, will communicate directly to the executive about difficulties created by adopting a particular track or strategy. If staff members apart from other executives mention problems at all, they tend to gloss over them for fear of alienating their bosses and losing their jobs.

Coaches are much more likely to speak frankly, because it is their responsibility to detect problems and make their clients aware of them. If people knew how to spot CEOs headed for failure - even if the company s results still looked fine - they could save themselves much pain. Trouble is, they usually look in the wrong direction (Charan & Colvin, 1999, p. 68).

What is Executive Coaching?

Coaching is "not a subset of management, but rather the heart of management" (Evered & Selman, 1989, p. 18). It's an ongoing, specific, and both short and long range process (Kroeger, 1991). It is a continuous process of improvement in the technical and people sides of any business (Stone & Stowell, 1990).

Birch (2002, p. 1) defined executive coaching as "a systematic approach to improvement through questioning and guidance that focuses on incremental changes in current performance to reach a target level." And in the business world, where victory "is garnered by those with the courage to push themselves to the very edge of their capability," Burdett claimed that coaching remains "the secret weapon of many outstanding organizations" (1998, p. 142).
Carter (2001) defined executive coaching as:

An interactive process that is designed to help individuals to develop rapidly. It is usually work related and focused on improving performance or behavior. It is a goal-oriented form of personal tailored learning for a busy executive. Coaching offers feedback and objectivity that cannot easily be gained from within the organization. (p. 11)

Responding to a 1999 survey carried out in the United Kingdom by *The Journal of Management Development*, a senior executive defined executive coaching as "a gift and a positive and energizing experience which above all enables an executive to shake off what may in fact be deeply held

automatic beliefs and behaviors that are inhibiting
performance and career development" (p. 2).

From a different perspective, O'Shaughnessy (2001)
defined coaching as:

> The route to liberating not only the full potential of
> careers, but also the full potential of an organization.
> It is exciting, fulfilling and it takes organizations to
> new realms of achievement. Like sports, coaching, too,
> focuses not only on technical issues, but also on
> psychological considerations. The executive and the
> coach will work together to identify areas of strength
> that can be used more effectively, blind spots in self-
> awareness and areas of weakness that need to be managed
> better. (p. 196)

Coaching is a process that "requires the very best from
all aspects of our humanity. It is not a path for the weak-
hearted or for people who are afraid to grow. It is a path
for the courageous and for people who are committed to
making a difference in the lives of those they touch
through coaching" (Crane, 1998, p. 215).

Although the two are related, coaching is different
from consulting (Table 1). Consulting focuses on business
formulas and gives external directions for executives to
follow for better business results. However, executive

coaching works with the executives internal strengths and
weaknesses to overcome their weaknesses and better utilize
their strengths.

Table 1

Differentiating Executive Coaching From Other Processes

Features Process	Originating tradition	Primary concern	Focus
Executive Coaching	Sports	• Solutions • Action • Individual performing better in the present	Rapid acquisition of knowledge, skills and behavior
Psychotherapy	Social	• Understanding past experiences and current ways of behaving • Reflection	Dealing with long-standing emotional issues, thoughts and ways of behaving
Counseling	Social	• Preventing negative aspects from individual s past inhibiting future performance	Coming to terms with event(s)
Mentoring	Apprenticeship	• Preparation • Individuals performing better in the future	Enhancing networking and career progression
Organization Development	Change	• Processes preventing team and organization performance	Rapid implementation and adaptation to change

Note. From Executive Coaching: Inspiring performance at work, by A.
Carter, 2001, The Institute for Employment Studies. Copyright 2001 by
A. Carter. Reprinted with permission.

While consulting provides business reports and
instructions, executive coaching changes the way people
think (Hargrove, 1995). Coaching in its several techniques
and approaches doesn t point out solutions; instead, it

inspires executives to make the right decisions in the first place, building on their ability to solve problems and prosper in the business.

Finally, James Flaherty of Coaching Connection defined coaching in a few strong words: "coaching is not about teaching the caterpillar how to fly; it's about creating an opening for it to see the possibility (1997, p. 2).

Is There a Real Need for Executive Coaching?

The need for executive coaching appears with particular clarity in Ram Charan s article Why CEOs Fail published in *Fortune* (June, 1999). Charan focused on executives simple, but often fatal, slips or mistakes. A good example would be the case of Eckhard Pfeiffer with Compaq Corporation.

Pfeiffer transformed the company more than once, multiplying Compaq s revenues, profits, and market value a remarkable achievement. However, Compaq s board of directors removed Pfeiffer for lack of vision regarding the Internet. Pfeiffer had to go because of a strategy that appeared to pull the company in the opposite direction (Charan & Colvin, 1999, p. 68).

In the same article, Charan stated that CEOs blame the following traps that toppled them off the pyramid: lack of feedback, looking in the wrong direction, failure to hold people accountable, failure to fire people at the right time, blind confidence in self-appointed subordinates, overlooking tiny but critical details, market denial, and getting stuck with one consulting or information source.

Charan added that there are five signs of failure that every CEO is advised to heed. These signs are performance, focus on the basics of execution, reliability of an information source, top subordinates bailing out before the CEO, and whether or not the board of executives is doing what it should.

The article also disclosed six habits of highly ineffective CEOs: people problems, decision gridlock, lifer syndrome, bad earning news, missing in action, and off the deep end financials. Each one of these habits is a strong reason to hire an executive coach.

Stuhlmann (2000) claimed that there are six reasons behind executives' failure. These include: failure to build partnerships with subordinates; confusion of position expectations; lack of political savvy; inability to achieve critical objective(s); taking too long to learn their jobs; and lack of balance between work and their own personal life.

Other factors, according to Stuhlmann, that contribute to such failure include: poor situational analysis, staying in one's comfort zone, inability to adapt to organizational and people differences, becoming overwhelmed, and inability to make tough decisions.

In the late 1980s, many executives from the United States and the United Kingdom realized that the recession left them with higher expectations, less time, and fewer resources to achieve their objectives. As most of their support staff was laid off, executives began looking for coaches who would go beyond mere consulting roles to point out troubles and personal issues that might jeopardize the tremendous expectations.

Personal development, people skills, decision-making, and real feedback are only a few of many areas in which executives need help. And since the recession had left them with drastically reduced staff and support, the need for the executive coach emerged. Literature from the United Kingdom and from the United States corroborates the trend.

Besides the aid coaching provides with soft skills such as people skills, it helps executives "navigate through the murky political, technological, and behavioral waters" (Cramm & May, 1998, p. 196).

Carter (2000) of the British Institute of Employment Studies (IES) claimed that:

Over 80 per cent of UK-based employers are using
mentoring, coaching, or one-to-one collaborative
processes to support individuals and improve
organization performance. By far the fastest area of
growth over the last three years is investment in
executive coaching for senior managers and top
specialists. This is becoming a mainstream activity in
organizations and driving a booming industry among
external coaches. (p. 1)

In her report, Carter gave the United States the credit
for exploring this service:

Executive coaching is an import from the U.S. that has
grown enormously in popularity across Europe in the few
years. Fees of around £2,000 per day for executive
coaches are not uncommon. This compares with an average
daily fee of £975 per day among British management
consultants. (p. 4)

The IES's findings were supported by results of a survey
that was published by the *Journal of Management Development*
in 1999. The survey found that:

Executive coaching is playing a major role in improving
the caliber of United Kingdom businesses and in
maximizing competitiveness . One senior respondent to
the survey estimates that she was able to bring more

than £15 million of added value to her organization

through new initiatives which coaching inspired her to

undertake. (p. 1)

Responding to a similar executive coaching survey

accomplished by *the Industrial and Commercial Training*

Group (O'Shaughnessy, 2001, p. 196), a senior executive

from the United Kingdom wrote:

I think we can learn from the U.S., where people are

actually often proud to admit that they are being

coached because they see it as indicating the importance

their employers attach to them. In the U.S. it is taken

for granted that performance will improve significantly

as a result of coaching.

Bloch (1995) argued that even the smartest top

executives cannot always take care of themselves. They may

need a range of development opportunities in areas of

interpersonal relationships, achieving a flexible

management style, and managing teams of subordinates.

Phillips (1995) claimed that executive coaching

creates the environment that enables people to perform to

the best of their abilities. In a similar vein, Ford (1992,

p. 1) argued that:

Coaching can help to manage relationships, improve self-

awareness of personal impact, and unlock oneself from

rigid ways of perceiving others and their problems. It is particularly relevant for isolated top management because managers need someone with whom they can communicate and discuss ideas without fear of organizational or career repercussions.

Hicks and Peterson (1996) claimed that coaching is a necessity in today's changing environment. In order for people to succeed in such environment, they have to adapt to these changes in a timely manner simply because they form the main source of competitive advantage.

In 2000, Betsy Morris reported to *Fortune* magazine the case of Mary Bradford, a sales manager of Metropolitan Life. Morris claimed that Bradford's first year of coaching "was like a grenade that's still going off . It taught her that people have to take more responsibility for their own growth and development. They can't depend on human resources" (p. 145). Morris also quoted John Kotter, a professor of leadership at Harvard Business School, saying that "as we move from 30 miles an hour to 70 to 120 to 180 as we go from driving straight down the road to making right turns and left turns, to abandoning cars and motorcycles the whole game changes, and a lot of people are trying to keep up, learn how, not to fall off" (p. 146).

Trust is another motive behind hiring executive coaches. In 1997, *Management Development Review* approached the trust issue, stating that "the higher up the managerial ladder a person gets, the fewer people there are around with whom he or she can communicate on a trusting, confidential basis" (p. 137).

The absence of necessary resources, like mentors, also plays a major role in hiring executive coaches. Carter (2001) claimed that the trend of flatter organizations is resulting in more isolated managers who in turn will seek "individually tailored development such as executive coaching" (p. 5).

During recession times, when more is expected from fewer managers (Barry, 1994), coaching stands out as a life ring in the middle of a storm-tossed environment (Bagshaw, 1997). It empowers individuals and organizations to survive by enhancing their skills, problem solving abilities, and adaptability to change (Tao & Wright, 2001).

The need for better soft skills is another reason behind the booming of executive coaching. Soft skills, those skills needed in today's leadership approaches other than technical ones, include gaining trust, developing people, empowering subordinates, enhancing relationships, and improving communications. Carter (2001) claimed that executive coaching is popular in the United Kingdom because of its ability to improve on soft skills.

Achieving balance between different areas of management is another reason behind hiring a coach. Blakenham (1993) claimed that "chairmen need to achieve balance between setting appropriate company values and strategic objectives" (p. 1). And Kippenberger (1997) stated that chief executive officers in their first days in the office also need to balance company goals with personal goals, expectations, teams, and short and long term objectives.

Surviving a fast changing business environment may also involve calling on executive coaches for help. Diamante, Giglio, and Urban (1998) argued that "organizations often provide a coach for executives who are having trouble with change and are in need of more effective leadership strategies. Coaching helps the executive focus on objectives, develop resiliency, and build interpersonal savvy" (p. 93). Carter (2001, p. 17) added that coaching helps during "the transition period, enabling the individual to be up and running in their new post as quickly as possible."

Executive coaching helps executives see alternative behaviors in their activities (Frankel & Otazo, 1992), and enables them to gain greater competence, and overcome barriers to improve performance (Lawson, 1992). Covey (1989, p. 207) added that coaching is a process that produces "ah-hah" or "I never thought of it like that" reactions.

O'Shaughnessy (2001, p. 195) stated that "executive coaching is one of the most powerful strategic and tactical weapons open to businesses today because of its ability to enhance areas of executive expertise that were already at a high level and to establish skills that were previously absent or weak." Executive coaching helps executives bridge the gap between their current skills and skills needed in the future (Drucker, 1989).

Coca-Cola Foods viewed coaching (Veale & Wachtel, 1996, p. 16) as a process that "helps the person increase competence and probability of success. Coaching can occur down the hierarchy, up it, or laterally. In coaching, the relationship is not of utmost importance, rather the agreement that the coaching is valuable is the critical element." Coaching offers a non-confrontational, confidence-building approach which forms the basis of a win-win situation.

In 1997, the *Management Development Review* reported that "there are more than 1,000 coaches working full time in the

USA, and the number is rising fast. Enrollment at the Houston-based Coach University is doubling every 12 months" (p. 137). Two years later, Hall, Hollenbeck, and Otazo (1999, p. 39) claimed that the number of executive coaches in the United States alone has been estimated to be in the tens of thousands. And in year 2001, Buchen estimated the number of coaches to be around 30,000, making more than $30 billion in the United States.

The Executive Coaching Process

According to Vance Caesar of the Professional Coaching and Mentoring Association (personal communication, April 19, 2001) Executive coaching is not an easy profession. Those who knock on executive doors and introduce themselves as executive coaches have to be aware of the tremendous responsibility of the profession. Vance Caesar (1999, p. 1) of the Professional Coaching and Mentoring Association (PCMA) of Southern California stated:

You might feel drawn to the idea of becoming a professional coach or mentor because you have significant experience in your specialty and you have enjoyed coaching and mentoring others. While you might enjoy using your particular expertise, success in becoming a professional coach or mentor requires more than just expertise in your field and having taken a few courses in coaching and/or mentoring. As with starting and building any other kind of business, coaching requires not only the desire to own and run your own business, but a wide range of management and business skills as well. A solid understanding of financial systems and coaching techniques and, perhaps even more important, an ability to market and sell your services competitively are all-important.

Carter (2001) stated that an effective coaching process should proceed according to the following six steps: entry and contracting, clarification of objectives, reaching shared diagnosis, taking action, and closure (Figure 2 & 3).

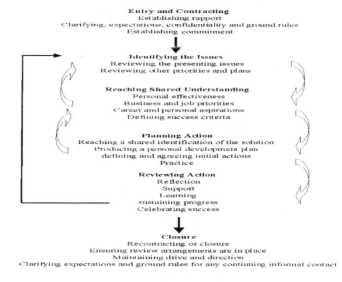

Figure 2. The six phases in executive coaching process. *Note.* From Executive Coaching: Inspiring performance at work, by A. Carter, 2001, The Institute for Employment Studies. Copyright 2001 by A. Carter. Reprinted with permission.

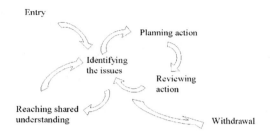

Figure 3.   The executive coaching process,
              from the coach's perspective.
Note. From Executive Coaching: Inspiring performance at work, by
A. Carter, 2001, The Institute for Employment Studies. Copyright
2001 by A. Carter. Reprinted with permission.

Phillips (1995) called coaching effective when it

creates an environment with the attributes of flexibility,

creativity, adaptability, responsibility, and availability

of trust and honesty. McNutt and Wright (1995, p. 28) stated

that "honesty is the best policy" between a coach and a

coachee, and Carter claimed that trust is the heart of

coaching (Figure 4).

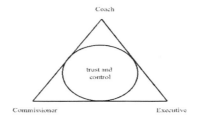

Figure 4. The executive coaching relationship triangle.
Note. From Executive Coaching: Inspiring performance at work, by
A. Carter, 2001, The Institute for Employment Studies. Copyright
2001 by A. Carter. Reprinted with permission.

Carter added that under each objective (personal,

business, career), there is a successful or effective

coaching process, addressed in Figure 5 below.

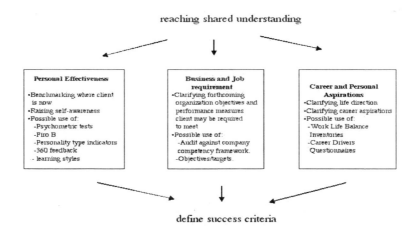

Figure 5. Reaching a shared understanding.
Note. From Executive Coaching: Inspiring performance at work, by
A. Carter, 2001, The Institute for Employment Studies. Copyright
2001 by A. Carter. Reprinted with permission.

Diamante et al. (1998) claimed that an effective executive coach is one who is aware of his or her client's emotional and psychological cues. Listening and focusing on appropriate information are no less important.

Effective coaching, according to Fiano (2002, p. 1), occurs when the coach "combines the best characteristics of a knowledgeable mentor, a business savvy consultant, an exacting teacher, and a trustworthy friend."

Hicks and Peterson (1995) argued that executive coaching becomes effective when feedback stays within the boundaries of the coaching objectives and priorities. However, feedback should go beyond the facts of the current situation to a plan of what one "could do the same or differently in the future" (p. 61).

Campbell, Mead, and Milan (1999, p. 283) called executive coaching effective and result oriented only when the coach works with his or her client's "whole person and takes a client-centered approach."

White and Whitherspoon (1998) defined effective executive coaching as a process that pinpoints the objective(s) of hiring a coach and stays on track until that goal is accomplished. Objectives include coaching for skills, performance, development, and the executive's agenda.

Lombardi (1992) said that the elements of effective executive coaching are vision, mental toughness, motivation, synergy, trust and respect, commitment, winning tradition, and winning attitude. And Odiorne (1991) defined effective coaching as a process that defines the gap between the current behavior and the sought behavior, and produces a strategy strong enough to bridge the gap.

Lipshitz and Popper (1992) argued that an effective executive coach is one that is able to perform the following four tasks during the coaching session: identify parameters of success, create a successful coaching environment, identify factors which lead to success, and identify inner sources of success.

Rosenberg (1992) keyed effective executive coaching to the following sequence: observe behavior, discuss that behavior immediately with the coachee, ask leading questions, and drive the coachee to commit to do something differently before the next coaching session.

Burdett (1998, p. 144) argued that in order for coaching to be effective, its agenda must reflect a strong appreciation of the context, including "the organization's mission, strategic intent, beliefs, and values." Burdett added that in order for the coaching process to be successful, the client must have the will to change, the capability to act in the way agreed on, and an opportunity to practice the new behavior. On top of that, a supportive climate or coaching environment is required (Redshaw, 2000).

Blanchard (1991) defined effective executive coaching technique as one that carries out day-to-day feedback, and Capozzoli (1993) called coaching effective when its timing is correct, when it focuses on outcome, and when it doesn't mix positive and negative feedback together.

Other aspects of effective coaching include open communication (Finn, 1991), non-judgmental listening (Gaines, 1993), open-ended questioning (Kinlaw, 1993), leading through expectations rather than command and control (Yager, 1993), and a powerful relationship between the coach and the coachee (Avidlsen & Weintraub, 1984).

Although some executives link effective executive coaching with practical experience and others give the coach more credibility if his or her experience matches theirs, few link good coaching with gender. But Carter (2001, p. 35) suggested that "it is not as important for a coach to know the details of a particular field as it is important to understand how business, in the broadest sense, works, and have the ability to coach the executive sensitively towards his or her goals."

Finally, for an executive coach to be effective, he or she has to assess or define the executive need(s), walk the executive throughout the stages of the process, and define the appropriate strategy and style that best fit the subject coachee.

Assessment of Areas That Need Coaching

In 1999, James Flaherty introduced a very effective model called the Five Elements Model to assess the area in which executives need coaching the most. The model surveys five areas: immediate concern or the most pressing problem; commitments, where the executive dedicates and allocates the most resources; future possibilities of achievements and strategies; personal and cultural history with people and the mode of response; and the executive's mood judgement, action and self-esteem.

Stages of Executive Coaching Process

Pryor (1994) claimed the following as the main stages of the executive coaching process:

1. Recognition of the need, when the executive realizes the need for improving personal or career effectiveness.

2. Contact, the stage at which the human resources or any other authority or person approaches the executive and informs him or her of the need.

3. Buy-in stage of realizing the need for improvement, and agreeing to work on the issue.

4. Gathering information seen necessary for the success of the coaching process.

Once the need for coaching service is realized and a contract is established, it is up to the coach to enact the proper coaching strategy.

Executive Coaching Strategies

Bergquist (1999) argued that all clients or executives are different, and that for each one there is a perfect coaching strategy. He added that it's the coach's responsibility to find out at an early stage what strategy best suits his or her coachee. Bergquist suggested that successful strategies focus on the client's unique functions and distinctive competencies, encourage executives to assist one another, and acknowledge a client's experience and expertise. Within each strategy, different styles can be deployed.

Executive Coaching Styles

Once a strategy is adopted, the coach chooses a coaching style that best fits the area of concern. Coca-Cola

(Veale & Wachtel, 1996), for example, uses five different types or styles of coaching: modeling, instructing, enhancing performance, problem solving and inspiration, and support.

In modeling, the coach has to have the skills he or she is trying to pass on to the client. In instructing, the coach starts with the overall picture then draws connections between that picture and individual tasks showing the importance of the client's job. Enhancing is all about improving performance. Problem solving is self-explanatory, and inspiration revolves around analogies from sports and strategies that get the best out of capable people simply by inspiring them.

Kimsey-House, Whitworth, and Sandahl (1998) introduced six coaching styles to match the variety of situations, environments, and differences among clients. These styles of coaching include coactive, reflective, appreciative, contextual, instrumented, and observational.

Coactive coaching. Coactive coaching incorporates four main points:

- The client is naturally creative and resourceful.
- The whole life of the client is addressed.
- The agenda comes from the client.

- The relationship between the coach and the coachee is that of an alliance.

Coactive coaching creates a relationship between the coach and his or her client. This relationship should be powerful enough to make the client a focal point with the full authority to set forth the coaching agenda. Kimsey-House et al. (1998, p. 13) suggested that, "the process of designing the alliance is a model of the mutual responsibility of client and coach. Clients learn that they are in control of the relationship and ultimately of the changes they make in their lives."

Reflective coaching. The concept of the reflective coaching style is built on the client's own reflections concerning his or her strengths and weaknesses. Reflective coaching is "very effective when used with two or more executives, particularly if they often work together and wish to reflect on their working relationship" (Bergquist, 1999, p. 117). One of the most important areas reflective coaching deals with is communication.

Appreciative coaching. From its title, it is obvious that appreciative coaching appreciates clients and their experience. Clients are experienced and talented enough and to solve their problems on their own. However, their environment, life, and endless agendas prevent them from gathering their strengths and solving their dilemmas. An appreciative coach is one that engages with those clients in a dialogue with an "assumption of mutual respect and mutual research for discovery of distinctive competencies and strengths" (Bergquist, 1999, p. 9).

Contextual coaching. The contextual coaching style classifies executives as assertive, inspiring, thoughtful, and participating (Bergquist, 1999). Each one of those classifications has its own style of coaching. Assertive executives are those known to be powerful and authoritative. Inspiring executives carry out decisions made by assertive people by inspiring the organization to respond in an appropriate manner. Inspiring executives make people look ahead. In this situation, the need for those who calculate risks and carefully study the next step becomes a necessity. Risk calculation is the primary function of the thoughtful executive. Participating executives are those who motivate the entire organization to get involved in achieving the desired goals. Shifting executives among these four roles and drawing boundaries for each role is the primary responsibility of the coach.

Instrument and observational coaching. Instrument and observational styles of coaching can be found within the coaching styles discussed above. Whether employing instruments like Myers-Briggs, General Electric s 360 feedback, or observes executives' behavior as a feedback, the coach is using a tool to gather information believed necessary for the chosen coaching style.

External Versus Internal Coaches

Carter (2000, p.1) argued that "organizations are switching from external to internal provision of executive coaching services to reduce cost and improve alignment with corporate strategy." However, Cramm and May (1998, p. 197) believed that "coaches are most effective when they are external to the organization you need someone who has a perspective that is more objective."

Carter also claimed that:

> There is no uncertainty or divided opinion, however, on the need for trust between the coach and the coached executive the executive needs to be certain that his weaknesses and concerns are not going to be broadcast to his peers or the organization in general. External coaches with no axe to grind in the internal politics of an organization are seen as particularly valuable for this very reason. (p. 35)

Smith (1993, p. 126) defined the executive coach as "an outside counselor assigned to improve the executive's managerial skills and straighten out a personality disorder."

Diamante et al. (1998, p. 94) defended the idea of hiring external coaches:

A coach is an outside individual who can take a fresh perspective and approach when analyzing organizational processes and one who has nothing to gain by taking a position. This is critical to the success of the endeavor, because many times the person in danger may not realize that he/she is in danger, or may not realize the severity of the problem.

Hall et al. (1999) argued that no comparison can be made between external and internal coaches simply because they each have their own niche. External coaches "are preferable when extreme confidentiality and anonymity are required and when someone is needed to speak the unspeakable" (p. 39). And "internal coaches are preferred when knowing the company culture and politics is critical, when easy availability is desired, and when personal trust and comfort are at a premium" (p. 40).

Selecting The Right Coach

According to Carter (2001), selecting the appropriate coach consists of two main steps: identifying a pool of coaches suitable for the business; and matching the executive and the coach based on the executive s needs, the coach's ability to fulfill those needs, and a personality fit between coach and executive.

Finally, in 1997 the *Management Development Review* advised executives seeking coaches to look out for a good personal manner, coaches with coaching experience, and those with knowledge of the executive's particular industry.

Summary of The Literature Review

Although the literature has discussed in detail the nature, benefits, and techniques of coaching, it has shed little light on the CEOs perceptions of executive coaching. Do CEOs believe in coaching? How do they deal with coaches? Do they feel discomfort when people find out about their coaching relationship? Where do they shop for a coach? And because the review has failed to show substantial research concerning the perception of executive coaching in the United States, this study was designed to fill the gap.

The following chapter deals with the design of the study and the validation of the instrument that was used in collecting data.

Chapter 3

Research Design

Introduction

The executive world is reluctant to respond to academic studies and surveys. However, the need to know the executives' perception of executive coaching made this study a necessity as well as a challenge. In order to visit their world and get the questions of this study answered, it was necessary that the whole process be clear and expedited. Based on this criterion, the study was designed.

Design of The Study

The study was designed to utilize a survey instrument to capture the CEOs perception of executive coaching. The survey consisted of 12 questions related to understanding and evaluation of coaching as a service offered at the CEOs level.

Population

Chief Executive Officers of America's top 500 companies, as listed on Fortune's April 15, 2002 issue, were the main population of this study. For the purpose of generalizing the outcomes of this study among the entire population, a minimum sample size of 218 with a confidence level of 95% and a margin of error of -/+5 was required (Booth-Kewley, Edwards, Rosenfeld, and Thomas, 1997). Since the response rate did not reach this minimum, a proportional analysis concept was utilized.

Sampling

According to Booth-Kewley, in order for the outcome(s) to be generalized among the largest 500 American companies, a minimum sample size of 218 is required. The number 218 represents the required responses and not the administered ones. The administered number was higher because of the ineligibles (CEOs who chose not to respond, and CEOs who were not available to respond). According to Kewley, the administered number was calculated as follows:

$$n' = n \ / \ (e) \ (r)$$

Where *n'* is the administered number, *n* is the minimum sample size, (e) is the confidence level (availability of the targeted), and (r) as the expected response rate (46% in this case). Doing the calculations, the number of surveys needed to be sent out was calculated as follows:

$$218/ \ (0.95 \ * \ 0.46) \ = \ 499$$

Therefore, the survey was sent to the entire population (see Appendix A for full list).

Data Collection Method

Instrument Background

To measure executives perception of coaching in America's top 500 companies, this study adapted an instrument, consisting of 12 questions, which was previously used to gather opinions about the use of biochemical in the north east coast of the United States. Permission to modify and use the instrument was obtained from Dr. William Hallman of the Human Ecology of Cook College, the State University of New Jersey (see Appendix C for authorizations).

Instrument Design

In a Likert scale format, the questionnaire measures the subject s knowledge of and extent of agreement with the use of executive coaching at the CEO level. Part one of the questionnaire targets the CEO s basic understanding of executive coaching. Part two was designed to measure the extent of his or her willingness to hire an executive coach. Part three discusses the CEO s preferences about the settings and the environment of the coaching sessions. Part four concludes with the CEO s opinion about the future of this service and whether or not support for executive coaching should continue. The questionnaire was designed to be completed by circling the appropriate level of agreement on an agree-disagree Likert scale.

Instrument Reliability

Reliability was assessed by estimates of the stability of scores over time and by using an alternate form. In assessing stability of scores over time, a test-retest procedure was employed in which 10 high rank management employees from the Boeing Company were asked to answer the same survey over a period of three weeks. The correlation between the two scores resulted in a reliability range of 0.66 to 0.94.

A high level of correlation was also reported between alternate forms of the instrument (0.62 to 0.97). Such a high range of correlation indicated a high level of reliability.

Instrument Validity

To assess the validity of the instrument, a panel of four experts was asked to review the questionnaire. The panel included Cindy Malawy, mentoring professional with the Boeing Company; David Buttson, executive coach with the Boeing Company; Dr. James McMunigal of Boeing s research and development; and Alison Carter of the British Institute of Employment Studies. The instrument was modified and adjusted in accordance with the panel s recommendations. While some recommendations focused on the use of words, others concentrated on the sequence and the flow. All modifications were carried out before the reliability tests were performed. Table 2 illustrates a comprehensive match between the research and instrument questions.

Table 2

Survey Questions Responding To Research Questions

Research Question	Survey Question
<u>1.1</u> What proportion of CEOs of America s top 500 companies are aware of executive coaching services?	• Q1 - How would you rate your own understanding of executive coaching?
<u>1.2</u> Of CEOs who are aware of executive coaching, what proportion are able to distinguish coaching from consulting?	• Q2 - Executive coaching is different from consulting (True/False).
<u>1.3</u> What proportion of CEOs believe in the benefits of executive coaching?	• Q3 - Based on what you know or have heard, will executive coaching as a paid-for service (like consulting) make the quality of CEOs better or worse?
<u>1.4</u> What proportion of CEOs are willing to hire an executive coach?	• Q.4 - Do you agree or disagree with CEOs hiring coaches? • Q.5 - Have you ever hired a coach? • Q.6 - If you answered with NO , would you be very willing to hire an executive coach?
<u>1.5</u> When hiring a coach, do CEOs prefer coaches from outside their organization?	• Q.7 - If you re hiring an executive coach, do you prefer outsiders or insiders?
<u>1.6</u> What proportion of CEOs prefer to keep the entire coaching process confidential?	• Q.9 - On average, CEOs don't like the public to know about their executive coaching relationship (True/False)
<u>1.7</u> What channels do CEOs use to hire coaches?	• Q.8 - When hiring a coach, where do you look for one?
<u>1.8</u> What proportion of CEOs believe that executive coaching should be limited to a particular management level?	• Q.11 - Should coaching be limited to a particular management level?
<u>1.9</u> What proportion of CEOs have preferences as to location where coaching sessions should be conducted?	• Q.10 - It s better for CEOs undergoing coaching, to have their coaching sessions conducted: on-site, off-site
<u>1.10</u> What proportion of CEOs support research for executive coaching?	• Q.12 - Should research and support for executive coaching continue?

Procedure

To respond to the research questions, the following procedures or steps were closely followed. The questionnaire along with a cover letter (Appendices B and D) were mailed to the CEOs of the top 500 companies (Appendix A). A cover letter explained the importance of the study and the participants critical role in the process.

Participants were assured full anonymity and were promised a copy of the findings. In order to get a higher response rate, an additional set of 300 letters was sent out to those who did not respond the first time.

Data then were gathered, tabulated, and analyzed using basic strategies of descriptive statistics, including the concept of proportion. Conclusions and recommendations were based on the highest percentages of the responses.

Protection of Human Subjects' Consideration

Recipients of the questionnaire were guaranteed absolute protection of the human subjects consideration. The cover letter guaranteed the anonymity and confidentiality of the subject s responses (Appendix D). No questions were asked that might reveal the identity of the respondent.

Once responses were received, data were analyzed using descriptive statistics tools.

Summary

This study was designed to explore the perception of executive coaching among the chief executive officers of

America's Fortune 500 companies. Data were gathered with a 12 item Likert type questionnaire. Stability of scores over time as well as the reliability of the instrument were assured through two alternate forms. A panel of four experts was charged with the test for validity. CEOs of the top 500 American companies, as listed in *Fortune 500* April 15, 2002, formed the study population. A total of 800 surveys was administered for the purpose of satisfying the minimum sample size of 218. A cover letter that offered participants a copy of the research findings along with protection of the human subjects consideration was mailed with the survey. Results were collected, coded, and analyzed using descriptive statistics process. The following chapter describes and interprets the findings of the study.

Chapter 4

Findings

Introduction

A survey of 12 questions was sent to the top 500 CEOs shown on Fortune s list of April 15, 2002 in order to explore their overall perception of executive coaching. A second set of 300 letters was sent to those who did not respond the first time. Of the total 500 surveyed CEOs, 143 returned the questionnaire (27%).

This chapter illustrates what the respondents had to say about the following: (a) their basic understanding of executive coaching, (b) their ability to differentiate executive coaching from consulting, (c) their belief in the benefits of executive coaching, (d) their level of willingness to hire a coach, (e) their preferences for either external or internal coaches, (f) whether they preferred keeping coaching relationships confidential, (g) where they preferred coaching sessions to be held, and (h) whether coaching should be limited to specific sectors of management.

Report of The Findings

Table 3

Survey Question 1: How Do CEOs Rate Their Basic Knowledge Of

Executive Coaching?

RESPONSE	FREQUENCY	PERCENTAGE
Very Good	45	31%
Adequate	64	45%
Poor	17	12%
Not Sure	17	12%
TOTAL	143	100%

The majority of the respondents (45%) rated their knowledge of executive coaching as adequate (Table 3). Fewer than a third (31%) claimed to have very good knowledge of the subject, and almost one fourth of the total respondents were divided between those with poor knowledge of executive coaching and those who were not sure.

Table 4

Survey Question 2: Is It True That Executive Coaching Is

Different From Consulting?

RESPONSE	FREQUENCY	PERCENTAGE
True	119	83%
False	14	10%
Not Sure	10	7%
TOTAL	143	100%

While a high percentage of the total responses (83%) differentiated coaching from consulting (Table 4), 10% thought they were the same; and a few (7%) were not sure.

Table 5

Survey Question 3: What Happens To The Quality Of CEOs Job Performance After Being Exposed To Executive Coaching?

RESPONSE	FREQUENCY	PERCENTAGE
Much Better	9	6%
Somewhat Better	78	55%
Somewhat Worse	19	13%
Much Worse	9	6%
Not Sure	28	20%
TOTAL	143	100%

Among the respondents, 55% believed that coaching would improve their job performance; 13% thought coaching would make it worse; 12% were divided between the two extremes (much better, much worse); and the balance, 20%, were not sure.

Table 6

Survey Question 4: Do CEOs Think That Hiring A Coach Is A Good Idea?

RESPONSE	FREQUENCY	PERCENTAGE
Strongly Agree	9	6%
Agree	60	43%
Disagree	36	26%
Strongly Disagree	9	6%
Not Sure	26	19%
TOTAL	140	100%

Forty-three percent of the total respondents agreed that hiring an executive coach is a good idea; 26% disagreed; 12% were divided between the extreme ends (strongly agree, strongly disagree); and 19% were not sure.

Table 7

Survey Question 5: Have The Participants Ever Hired An Executive Coach?

RESPONSE		FREQUENCY	PERCENTAGE
Yes		46	32%
No		97	68%
	TOTAL	143	100%

Forty-six CEOs out of the total 143 who participated (32%) said they had hired a coach, while ninety-seven (68%) had not (Table 7).

Table 8

Survey Question 6: Are CEOs Who Never Hired An Executive Coach Willing To Hire One?

RESPONSE		FREQUENCY	PERCENTAGE
Very Willing		9	9%
Somewhat Willing		27	28%
Not Very Willing		26	27%
Not At All Willing		35	36%
	TOTAL	97	100%

Fifty-five percent of those who never hired a coach (Tables 7 & 8) were split between those somewhat willing to hire a coach and those not very willing to do so. A small group of 9% expressed a strong willingness, and a little over one third (36%) completely rejected the idea of hiring an executive coach.

Table 9

Survey Question 7: Do CEOs Hiring Coaches Prefer Outsiders,

Insiders, Or Have No Preference?

RESPONSE		FREQUENCY	PERCENTAGE
Internal		11	8%
External		89	62%
No Preference		43	30%
	TOTAL	143	100%

Respondents who preferred coaches from outside their

companies outnumbered those preferring coaches from inside

as shown in the above table (62% versus 8% respectively). A

little under one third of the respondents (30%) had no

preference.

Table 10

Survey Question 8: When Hiring Coaches, Where Do CEOs Go To

Look For Them?

RESPONSE		FREQUENCY	PERCENTAGE
Human Resource		71	51%
Internet		19	14%
Friend		16	12%
Outside Consultant		32	23%
	TOTAL	138	100%

Table 10 indicates that a majority of the 138

respondents (51%) favored looking for a coach through human

resources; 23% preferred looking for one through outside

consultants; and 26% were split between using the Internet

and consulting a friend when searching for an executive

coach.

Table 11

Survey Question 9: Do CEOs Prefer To Keep Their Coaching Contracts Confidential?

RESPONSE	FREQUENCY	PERCENTAGE
True	62	43%
False	13	9%
Not Sure	68	48%
TOTAL	143	100%

Of the 143 who responded, 43% believed that CEOs who hire coaches do keep their relationship confidential. Nine percent opposed that belief, and almost half of the respondents (48%, Table 11) were not sure.

Table 12

Survey Question 10: Where Do CEOs Prefer Coaching Sessions Be Located?

RESPONSE	FREQUENCY	PERCENTAGE
In Person On Site	27	19%
In Person Off Site	45	31%
Over the Telephone	18	13%
No Preference	53	37%
TOTAL	143	100%

CEOs who have preferences as to where coaching should be conducted formed 63% of the total respondents. Of these, 19% preferred "in person-on site" coaching, 31% favored "in person-off site", and 13% selected "over the telephone"(Table 12).

Table 13

Survey Question 11: To What Sector Of Management Should

Executive Coaching Be Limited?

RESPONSE	FREQUENCY	PERCENTAGE
New CEOs	17	12%
Experienced CEOs	10	7%
Both	26	18%
Management Below CEOs	34	24%
Unlimited	56	39%
TOTAL	143	100%

Twenty-four percent of the 143 respondents said that
executive coaching should be limited to management below the
CEO level (Table 13), and 18% believed coaching should be
available for new and experienced CEOs. However, the largest
number of the participants (39%) thought that such a service
should not be limited.

Table 14

Survey Question 12: Do CEOs Support Research For Executive

Coaching?

RESPONSE	FREQUENCY	PERCENTAGE
Continue	53	37%
Stop	27	19%
Not Sure	63	44%
TOTAL	143	100%

Out of the 143 respondents, 37% supported research in
the executive coaching area, and 19% opposed the idea (Table
14). Sixty-three or 44%, neither supported nor opposed such
research.

Summary of the Findings

Out of the 500 targeted CEOs, 143 participated in this study. Seventy-six percent of the respondents indicated adequate understanding of the basic concepts of executive coaching. Eighty-three percent were able to distinguish coaching from consulting, 61% believed that coaching could make their life somewhat better, 49% accepted the idea of hiring executive coaches, and 32% said they had hired one.

Those who never hired a coach showed a great deal of willingness (37%) to hire one. Sixty-two percent of the respondents preferred coaches from outside their organizations, 51% would search for one through human resources, 31% preferred sites off their company premises for coaching sessions, and 43% said they would keep their coaching relationship confidential.

Thirty-nine percent of the participants claimed that coaching should not be limited to a specific management level, and 37% said they were in support of research related to executive coaching.

The following chapter lays out recommendations based on these findings.

Chapter 5

Summary

This study was designed to explore the perception of executive coaching among America's top 500 CEOs. Areas under study included the CEOs' understanding of executive coaching as a service that differs from consulting, their awareness of the beneficial effects of executive coaching, their willingness to hire a coach, their preferences of where to look for a coach and where to hold the coaching sessions, their views on keeping the coaching relationship confidential, and whether research and coaching services should be limited to a certain sector of management. The target population consisted of the top 500 CEOs as listed in *Fortune*, April 15, 2002. Of the entire population surveyed, a response rate of 27% was achieved.

Respondents indicated a good understanding of the term "executive coaching," were able to distinguish it from consulting, agreed that hiring a coach was a good idea, preferred external coaches, had a preference for off-site coaching sessions, and supported research on coaching.

Conclusions and Recommendations

The following recommendations are for future studies as well as for executives, coaches, and companies currently involved with complex situations:

- Executives who have experienced coaching highly recommend the process. Their enthusiasm suggests there is a high return on the investment.

- Those who never hired a coach were somewhat reluctant to hire one. This outcome infers that more and better marketing campaigns are needed to make known the benefits of the service.

- Few participants were opposed to the idea of hiring a coach. That could mean something went wrong with the matching process.

- Between 1995 and 2002, both the number of executive coaches and the number of CEOs exposed to coaching in the United States increased dramatically, a phenomenon that suggests that there are benefits from investing in coaching.

- Matching the CEO with the right coach requires a background examination of the potential coach, including knowledge of his or her previous clients. It is important that the hiring CEO avoids coaches whose previous clients may have brought their companies down.

- The majority of the survey respondents indicated that their source of hiring coaches was human resources. A question remains, was this a coincidence? Or was it an indication of the restrictions companies place on their personnel in terms of whom to hire and how much to pay for coaching contracts?

- Many respondents prefer coaches from outside their companies. Companies are advised to respect that preference and not to mandate internal hiring.

- Most respondents prefer off-site locations for coaching sessions; companies are advised to accommodate these CEOs.

- CEOs believe that coaching should be within reach of every management level. Companies are advised to allocate time and budgets to make this happen.

- Coaches are advised to evaluate their ability to accommodate potential clients honestly before signing coaching contracts. Many coaches accept contracts even though their experience and skills fall short of fulfilling the commitment.

- Coaches are advised to keep their coaching contracts confidential and never use client names to market themselves.

- Coaches are advised to set different agendas for and to target different management levels. They are also advised to contract with organizations rather than with individuals for longer terms and more accessibility.

- Further studies may set up a national coach database that would match the client with the most appropriate coach, and keep track of the coaches' coaching histories in much the way credit bureaus keep track of people s credit histories. Clients names should be kept confidential except from authorized persons.

- Further studies may compare executive coaching with "trusted advisors." A trusted advisor is someone more closely related to a CEO than is an executive coach. Such individuals may often be more flexible and give much deeper feedback than coaches.

- Future studies could interview CEOs and other top executives to gain further understanding of how coaching sessions should be conducted and to determine whether the gender variable is significant.

- Further research could help an organization design a coaching department that would take care of most of its coaching needs.

- Further studies can also explore the difference between executive coaching and psychotherapy.

References

Avidlsen, J. (director), & Weintraub, J. (producer) (1984). *Karate kid* [film]. Burbank: Columbia Pictures.

Bagshaw, M. (1997). Coaching - not new but newly relevant. *Industrial and Commercial Training, 29* (5), 166-167.

Barry, T. (1994). How to be a good coach. *Management Development Review, 7* (4), 24-26.

Benton, D. (1996). *How to think like a CEO*. New York, NY: Warner Books, Inc.

Bergquist, W., Merritt, K., & Phillips, S. (1999). *Executive coaching: an appreciative approach*. Sacramento, CA: The Pacific Sounding Press.

Bianco, A., & Lavelle, L. (2000, December 11). The CEO trap. *BusinessWeek*, 87-96.

Birch, P. (2002). Instant coaching. *Emerald Library*. Retrieved April 4, 2002, from http://tamino.emerald-library.co cb/00438022/v50n7/s6005/p51.htm

Blakenham, V. (1993). What makes a good chairman and why it matters. *Executive Development, 6* (3).

Blanchard, K., & Blanchard, M. (1991). Managing performance. *Executive Excellence, 8* (11), 3-5.

Bloch, S. (1995). Coaching tomorrow's top managers. *Executive Development, 8* (5), 20-22.

Booth-Kewley, S., Edwards, J., Rosenfeld, P., & Thomas, M. (1997). *How to conduct organizational surveys*. Thousand Oaks, CA: Sage Publications, Inc.

Buchen, I. (2001). The inner circle of the trusted advisor. *Industrial and Commercial Training, 33* (3), 94-98.

Burdett, J. (1998). Forty things every manager should know about coaching. *Journal of Management Development, 17* (2), 142-152.

Caesar, V., & Harrison, H. (1999, March). *Professional coaching and mentoring, your road map to financial success*.

Paper presented at the meeting of the Professional Coaching and Mentoring Association on Executive Coaching, Orange County, CA.

Campbell, J., Mead, G., & Milan, M. (1999). Mentor and athene: supervising professional coaches and mentors. *Career Development International, 4* (5), 283-290.

Capozzoli, T. (1993). Developing productive employees. *Supervision, 54* (10), 16-17.

Carry on coaching? (1997). *Management Development Review, 10,* (4/5), 137-138.

Carter, A. (2000). *Making the most of executive coaching.* The Institute for Employment Studies Newsletter. Retrieved February 8, 2002, from http://www.employmnet-studies.co.uk/news/125art1.html

Carter, A. (2001). *Executive coaching: Inspiring performance at work* (Rep. No. 379). Brighton, UK: The Institute for Employment Studies.

Charan, R., & Colvin, G. (1999, June 21). Why CEOs fail. *Fortune, 139,* 68-70.

Covey, S. (1989). *The 7 habits of highly effective people.* New York, NY: Simon and Schuster.

Cramm, S., & May, T. (1998). Accelerating executive development: Hey coach . *Information Management & Security, 6* (5), 196-198.

Crane, T. (1998). *The heart of coaching.* San Diego, CA: FTA Press.

Dastrala, R, & McLarney, C. (2001). Socio-political structures as determinates of global success: the case of Enron Corporation. *International Journal of Social Economics, 28* (4), 349-367.

Diamante, T., Giglio, L., & Urban, J. (1998). Coaching a leader: leveraging change at the top. *The Journal Of Management Development, 17* (2), 93-105.

Drucker, P. (1989). *The new realities.* New York, NY: Harper & Row.

Evered, R., & Selman, J. (1989). Coaching and the art of *management. Organizational Dynamics, 18* (2), 16-32.

Executive coaching playing a crucially important role in UK business, survey finds (2001, October). *The Journal of Management Development.* Retrieved February 5, 2002 from http://haly.emeraldinsight.com/v cb/02621711/v20n5/s3001/p1I .htm

Executive coaching promises to address senior management skills gap (2001, March). *Industrial and Commercial Training.* Retrieved February 5, 2002, from http://haly.emeraldinsight.com/v cb/00197858/v33n7/s3002/p2I .htm

Fiano, R. (2002). Next generation leader: Coaching. *Organization & Leadership Development at The Boeing Corporation.* Retrieved April 23, 2002, from http://peopleweb.web.boeing.com/o&ld/y_NGL_Coacing.stm

Finn, W. (1991). One-on-one coaching. *Successful Meetings, 40* (8), 102-104.

Flaherty, J. (1997). Coaching and the new biology. *Coaching Connection.* Retrieved April 2, 2002. From http://leadership.gc.ca/static/coaching/documents/coaching_a nd_the_new_biology_e.shtml

Flaherty, J. (1999). *Coaching: evoking excellence in others.* Woburn, MA: Butterworth-Heinemann.

Ford, R. (1992). Professional coaching in leadership development. *Executive Development,5* (4).

Fortune, Company Profile (2002, January). New York, NY. *The Fortune Magazine.* Retrieved January 12, 2002, from http://www.fortune.com

Frankel, L., & Otazo, K. (1992). Employee coaching: the way to gain commitment, not just compliance. *Employment Relations Today*, 19 (3), 231-240.

Gaines, H. (1993). Ten tips for effective coaching. *Executive Excellence, 10* (3), 13.

Hall, d., Hollenbeck, G., & Otazo, K. (1999). Behind closed doors: what really happens in executive coaching. *American Management Association, Winter 1999*, 39-50.

Hallman, W. (1995). *Public perceptions of agricultural biotechnology*. Rutgers: The State University of New Jersey, Cook College, Department of Human Ecology.

Hargrove, R. (1995). *Masterful coaching*. San Francisco, CA: Josscy-Bass/Pfeiffer

Hicks, M., & Peterson, D. (1995). *Development first: strategies for self-development*. Minneapolis: Litho Incorporated.

Hicks, M., & Peterson, D. (1996). *Leader as coach*. Minneapolis: Litho Incorporated.

Kimsey-House, H., Whitworth, L., & Sandahl, P. (1998). *Co-Active coaching*. Palo Alto: Davies-Black Publishing.

Kinlaw, D. (1993). *Coaching for commitment*. Amsterdam, Netherlands: Pfieffer & Company.

Kippenberger, T. (1997). The first 100 days: the CEO's honeymoon period. *The Antidote*, *2* (3), 16-18.

Kroeger, L. (1991). Your team can't win the game without solid coaching. *Corporate Controller*, *3* (95), 62-64.

Lawson, K. (1992). First you train, then you coach. *Bottomline*, *9* (3), 34-35.

Lipshitz, R., & Popper, M. (1992). Coaching on leadership. *Leadership & Organization Development Journal*, *13* (7), 15-18.

Lombardi, V. (1992). Coaching for teamwork. *Executive Excellence*, *9* (4), 9-10.

McNutt, R., & Wright, P. (1995). Coaching your employees: applying sports analogies to business. *Executive Development, 8* (1), 27-32.

Morris, B. (February 21, 2000). So you're a player, do you need a coach? *Fortune*, 144-152.

Odiorne, G. (1991). Four magic moments in changing behavior. *Training, 28* (6), 43-46.

O'Shaughnessy, S. (2001). Executive coaching: the route to business stardom. *Industrial and Commercial Training, 33* (6), 194-197.

Phillips, R. (1995). Coaching for higher performance. Executive Development, *8* (7), 5-7.

Pryor, S. (1994). *Executive coaching: sign of success or stigma?* Boston: Boston University School of Management, Executive Development Roundtable.

Redshaw, B. (2000). Do we really understand coaching? How can we make it work better? *Industrial and Commercial Training, 32* (3), 106-108.

Rosenberg, D. (1992). Coaching without criticizing. *Executive Excellence, 9* (98), 14-15.

Smith, L. (1993). The executive's new coach. *Fortune, 128* (16), 126-134.

Stone, W., & Stowell, S. (1990). Coaching: The heart of management. *Executive Excellence, 7* (1), 8-9.

Stuhlmann, E. (2000, March). *An idea trend to think about today*. Exec.U.Net. Retrieved March 13, 2000, from http://www.execunet.com

Tao, F., & Wright, P. (2001). The missing link: coaching as a method of improving managerial skills in smaller businesses in Asia. *Career Development International, 6* (4), 218-225.

Veale, D., & Wachtel, J. (1996). Mentoring and coaching as part of a human resource development strategy: an example of Coca-Cola Foods. *Leadership & Organizational Development Journal, 17* (3), 16-20.

White, R., & Whitherspoon, R. (1998). *Four essential ways that coaching can help executives*. Greensboro: Center for Creative Leadership Publication.

Yager, E. (1993). Coaching models. *Executive Excellence, 10* (3), 18-19.

Appendices

Appendix A

List of The Population

WAL-MART **CEO:** H. Lee Scott Jr. **Address:** 702 S.W. Eighth St. Bentonville, AR 72716 **Phone:** 479-273-4000 **Website:** http://www.walmartstores.com	**DUKE ENERGY** **CEO:** Richard B. Priory **Address:** 526 S. Church St. Charlotte, NC 28202 **Phone:** 704-594-6200 **Website:** http://www.duke-energy.com	**CARDINAL HEALTH** **CEO:** Robert D. Walter **Address:** 7000 Cardinal Place Dublin, OH 43017 **Phone:** 614-757-5000 **Website:** http://www.cardinal.com	**SEARS ROEBUCK** **CEO:** Alan J. Lacy **Address:** 3333 Beverly Rd. Hoffman Estates, IL 60179 **Phone:** 847-286-2500 **Website:** http://www.sears.com
MOBIL **CEO:** Lee R. Raymond **Address:** 5959 Las Colinas Blvd. Irving, TX 75039 **Phone:** 972-444-1000 **Website:** http://www.exxonmobil.com	**AT&T** **CEO:** C. Michael Armstrong **Address:** 32 Sixth Ave. New York, NY 10013 **Phone:** 212-387-5400 **Website:** http://www.att.com	**MERCK** **CEO:** Raymond V. Gilmartin **Address:** 1 Merck Dr. Whitehouse Station, NJ 08889 **Phone:** 908-423-1000 **Website:** http://www.merck.com	**AQUILA** **CEO:** Robert K. Green **Address:** 20 W. Ninth St. Kansas City, MO 64105 **Phone:** 816-421-6600 **Website:** http://www.utilicorp.com
GM **CEO:** G. Richard Wagoner Jr. **Address:** 300 Renaissance Center Detroit, MI 48265 **Phone:** 313-556-5000 **Website:** http://www.gm.com	**BOEING** **CEO:** Philip M. Condit **Address:** 100 N. Riverside Plaza Chicago, IL 60606 **Phone:** 312-544-2000 **Website:** http://www.boeing.com	**STATE FARM INSURANCE** **CEO:** Edward B. Rust Jr. **Address:** 1 State Farm Plaza Bloomington, IL 61710 **Phone:** 309-766-2311 **Website:** http://www.statefarm.com	**TARGET** **CEO:** Robert J. Ulrich **Address:** 1000 Nicollet Mall Minneapolis, MN 55403 **Phone:** 612-304-6073 **Website:** http://www.target.com
FORD **CEO:** William Clay Ford Jr. **Address:** 1 American Rd. Dearborn, MI 48126 **Phone:** 313-322-3000 **Website:** http://www.ford.com	**EL PASO** **CEO:** William A. Wise **Address:** 1001 Louisiana St. Houston, TX 77002 **Phone:** 713-420-2600 **Website:** http://www.elpaso.com	**RELIANT ENERGY** **CEO:** R. Steve Letbetter **Address:** 1111 Louisiana St. Houston, TX 77002 **Phone:** 713-207-3000 **Website:** http://www.reliantenergy.com	**PROCTER & GAMBLE** **CEO:** Alan G. Lafley **Address:** 1 Procter & Gamble Plaza Cincinnati, OH 45202 **Phone:** 513-983-1100 **Website:** http://www.pg.com
ENRON **CEO:** Stephen F. Cooper **Address:** 1400 Smith St. Houston, TX 77002 **Phone:** 713-853-6161 **Website:** http://www.enron.com	**HOME DEPOT** **CEO:** Robert L. Nardelli **Address:** 2455 Paces Ferry Rd. N.W. Atlanta, GA 30339 **Phone:** 770-433-8211 **Website:** http://www.homedepot.com	**SBC COMMUNICATIONS** **CEO:** Edward E. Whitacre Jr. **Address:** 175 E. Houston St. San Antonio, TX 78205 **Phone:** 210-821-4105 **Website:** http://www.sbc.com	**MERRILL LYNCH** **CEO:** David H. Komansky **Address:** 4 World Financial Center New York, NY 10080 **Phone:** 212-449-1000 **Website:** http://www.ml.com
GE **CEO:** Jeffrey R. Immelt **Address:** 3135 Easton Turnpike Fairfield, CT 06431 **Phone:** 203-373-2211 **Website:** http://www.ge.com	**BANK OF AMERICA CORP.** **Address:** 100 N. Tryon St. Charlotte, NC 28255 **Phone:** 704-386-5000 **Website:** http://www.bankofamerica.com	**HEWLETT-PACKARD** **CEO:** Carleton S. Fiorina **Address:** 3000 Hanover St. Palo Alto, CA 94304 **Phone:** 650-857-1501 **Website:** http://www.hp.com	**AOL TIME WARNER** **CEO:** Richard D. Parsons **Address:** 75 Rockefeller Plaza New York, NY 10019 **Phone:** 212-484-8000 **Website:** http://www.aoltimewarner.com
CITIGROUP **CEO:** Sanford I. Weill **Address:** 399 Park Ave. New York, NY 10043 **Phone:** 212-559-1000 **Website:** http://www.citigroup.com	**FANNIE MAE** **CEO:** Franklin D. Raines **Address:** 3900 Wisconsin Ave. N.W. Washington, DC 20016 **Phone:** 202-752-7000 **Website:** http://www.fanniemae.com	**MORGAN STANLEY** **CEO:** Philip J. Purcell **Address:** 1585 Broadway New York, NY 10036 **Phone:** 212-761-4000 **Website:** http://www.msdw.com	**FREDDIE MAC** **CEO:** Leland C. Brendsel **Address:** 8200 Jones Branch Dr. McLean, VA 22102 **Phone:** 703-903-2000 **Website:** http://www.freddiemac.com
CHEVRON TEXACO **CEO:** David J. O'Reilly **Address:** 575 Market St. San Francisco, CA 94105 **Phone:** 415-894-7700 **Website:** http://www.chevron.com	**J.P. MORGAN CHASE** **CEO:** William B. Harrison Jr. **Address:** 270 Park Ave. New York, NY 10017 **Phone:** 212-270-6000 **Website:** http://www.jpmorganchase.com	**DYNEGY** **CEO:** Chuck L. Watson **Address:** 1000 Louisiana Suite 5800 Houston, TX 77002 **Phone:** 713-507-6400 **Website:** http://www.dynegy.com	**WORLDCOM** **CEO:** Bernard J. Ebbers **Address:** 500 Clinton Center Dr. Clinton, MS 39056 **Phone:** 601-460-5600 **Website:** http://www.worldcom.com
IBM **CEO:** Samuel J. Palmisano **Address:** New Orchard Rd. Armonk, NY 10504 **Phone:** 914-499-1900 **Website:** http://www.ibm.com	**KROGER** **CEO:** Joseph A. Pichler **Address:** 1014 Vine St. Cincinnati, OH 45202 **Phone:** 513-762-4000 **Website:** http://www.kroger.com	**MCKESSON** **CEO:** John H. Hammergren **Address:** 1 Post St. San Francisco, CA 94104 **Phone:** 415-983-8300 **Website:** http://www.mckesson.com	**MARATHON OIL** **CEO:** Clarence P. Cazalot Jr. **Address:** 5555 San Felipe Ave. Houston, TX 77253 **Phone:** 713-629-6600 **Website:** http://www.marathon.com

CONOCO **CEO:** Archie W. Dunham **Address:** 600 N. Dairy Ashford Houston, TX 77079 **Phone:** 281-293-1000 **Website:** http://www.conoco.com	**ALLSTATE** **CEO:** Edward M. Liddy **Address:** 2775 Sanders Rd. Northbrook, IL 60062 **Phone:** 847-402-5000 **Website:** http://www.allstate.com	**INTERNATIONAL PAPER** **CEO:** John T. Dillon **Address:** 400 Atlantic St. Stamford, CT 06921 **Phone:** 203-541-8000 **Website:** http://www.ipaper.com	**INGRAM MICRO** **CEO:** Kent B. Foster **Address:** 1600 E. St. Andrew Place Santa Ana, CA 92705 **Phone:** 714-566-1000 **Website:** http://www.ingrammicro.com
PFIZER **CEO:** Henry A. McKinnell **Address:** 235 E. 42nd St. New York, NY 10017 **Phone:** 212-573-2323 **Website:** http://www.pfizer.com	**TXU** **CEO:** Erle Nye **Address:** 1601 Bryan St. Dallas, TX 75201 **Phone:** 214-812-4600 **Website:** http://www.txu.com	**DELPHI** **CEO:** J. T. Battenberg III **Address:** 5725 Delphi Dr. Troy, MI 48098 **Phone:** 248-813-2000 **Website:** http://www.delphiauto.com	**LUCENT TECHNOLOGIES** **CEO:** Patricia F. Russo **Address:** 600 Mountain Ave. Murray Hill, NJ 07974 **Phone:** 908-582-8500 **Website:** http://www.lucent.com
J.C. PENNY **CEO:** Allen Questrom **Address:** 6501 Legacy Dr. Plano, TX 75024 **Phone:** 972-431-1000 **Website:** http://www.jcpenney.net	**UNITED TECHNOLOGIES** **CEO:** George David **Address:** 1 Financial Plaza Hartford, CT 06103 **Phone:** 860-728-7000 **Website:** http://www.utc.com	**SPRINT** **CEO:** William T. Esrey **Address:** 2330 Shawnee Mission Pkwy. Westwood, KS 66205 **Phone:** 913-624-3000 **Website:** http://www.sprint.com	**LOCKHEED MARTIN** **CEO:** Vance D. Coffman **Address:** 6801 Rockledge Dr. Bethesda, MD 20817 **Phone:** 301-897-6000 **Website:** http://www.lockheedmartin.com
METLIFE **CEO:** Robert H. Benmosche **Address:** 1 Madison Ave. New York, NY 10010 **Phone:** 212-578-2211 **Website:** http://www.metlife.com	**DOW CHEMICAL** **CEO:** Michael D. Parker **Address:** 2030 Dow Center Midland, MI 48674 **Phone:** 989-636-1000 **Website:** http://www.dow.com	**NEW YORK LIFE** **CEO:** Seymour G. Sternberg **Address:** 51 Madison Ave. New York, NY 10010 **Phone:** 212-576-7000 **Website:** http://www.newyorklife.com	**WALGREEN** **CEO:** David W. Bernauer **Address:** 200 Wilmot Rd. Deerfield, IL 60015 **Phone:** 847-940-2500 **Website:** http://www.walgreens.com
MIRANT **CEO:** S. Marce Fuller **Address:** 1155 Perimeter Center W. Atlanta, GA 30338 **Phone:** 678-579-7000 **Website:** http://www.mirant.com	**CONAGRA** **CEO:** Bruce C. Rohde **Address:** 1 ConAgra Dr. Omaha, NE 68102 **Phone:** 402-595-4000 **Website:** http://www.conagra.com	**DU PONT** **CEO:** Charles O. Holliday Jr. **Address:** 1007 Market St. Wilmington, DE 19898 **Phone:** 302-774-1000 **Website:** http://www.dupont.com	**BANK ONE COR.** **CEO:** James Dimon **Address:** 1 Bank One Plaza Chicago, IL 60670 **Phone:** 312-732-4000 **Website:** http://www.bankone.com
DELL COMPUTER **CEO:** Michael S. Dell **Address:** 1 Dell Way Round Rock, TX 78682 **Phone:** 512-338-4400 **Website:** http://www.dell.com	**PRUDENTIAL FINANCIAL** **CEO:** **Address:** 751 Broad St. Newark, NJ 07102 **Phone:** 973-802-6000 **Website:** http://www.prudential.com	**GEORGIA-PACIFIC** **CEO:** Alston D. Correll **Address:** 133 Peachtree St. N.E. Atlanta, GA 30303 **Phone:** 404-652-4000 **Website:** http://www.gp.com	**TIAA-CREF** **CEO:** John H. Biggs **Address:** 730 Third Ave. New York, NY 10017 **Phone:** 212-490-9000 **Website:** http://www.tiaa-cref.org
GOLDMAN SACHS GROUP **CEO:** Henry M. Paulson Jr. **Address:** 85 Broad St. New York, NY 10004 **Phone:** 212-902-1000 **Website:** http://www.gs.com	**PEPSICO** **CEO:** Steven S. Reinemund **Address:** 700 Anderson Hill Rd. Purchase, NY 10577 **Phone:** 914-253-2000 **Website:** http://www.pepsico.com	**MICROSOFT** **CEO:** Steven A. Ballmer **Address:** 1 Microsoft Way Redmond, WA 98052 **Phone:** 425-882-8080 **Website:** http://www.microsoft.com	**Phillips Petroleum** **CEO:** James J. Mulva **Address:** Phillips Bldg. Bartlesville, OK 74004 **Phone:** 918-661-6600 **Website:** http://www.phillips66.com
UNITED PARCEL SERVICE **CEO:** Michael L. Eskew **Address:** 55 Glenlake Pkwy. N.E. Atlanta, GA 30328 **Phone:** 404-828-6000 **Website:** http://www.ups.com	**WELLS FARGO** **CEO:** Richard M. Kovacevich **Address:** 420 Montgomery St. San Francisco, CA 94163 **Phone:** 800-411-4932 **Website:** http://www.wellsfargo.com	**WALT DISNEY** **CEO:** Michael D. Eisner **Address:** 500 S. Buena Vista St. Burbank, CA 91521 **Phone:** 818-560-1000 **Website:** http://www.disney.com	**BELL SOUTH** **CEO:** F. Duane Ackerman **Address:** 1155 Peachtree St. Atlanta, GA 30309 **Phone:** 404-249-2000 **Website:** http://www.bellsouth.com
MOTOROLA **CEO:** Christopher B. Galvin **Address:** 1303 E. Algonquin Rd. Schaumburg, IL 60196 **Phone:** 847-576-5000 **Website:** http://www.motorola.com	**INTEL** **CEO:** Craig R. Barrett **Address:** 2200 Mission College Blvd. Santa Clara, CA 95052 **Phone:** 408-765-8080 **Website:** http://www.intel.com	**AETNA** **CEO:** John W. Rowe M.D. **Address:** 151 Farmington Ave. Hartford, CT 06156 **Phone:** 860-273-0123 **Website:** http://www.aetna.com	**HONEYWELL INT.** **CEO:** David M. Cote **Address:** 101 Columbia Rd. Morristown, NJ 07962 **Phone:** 973-455-2000 **Website:** http://www.honeywell.com

UNITEDHEALTH GROUP **CEO:** William W. McGuire M.D. **Address:** 9900 Bren Rd. E. Minnetonka, MN 55343 **Phone:** 952-936-1300 **Website:** http://www.unitedhealthgroup.	**CVS** **CEO:** Thomas M. Ryan **Address:** 1 CVS Dr. Woonsocket, RI 02895 **Phone:** 401-765-1500 **Website:** http://www.cvs.com	**QWEST COMMUNICATIONS** **CEO:** Joseph P. Nacchio **Address:** 1801 California St. Denver, CO 80202 **Phone:** 303-992-1400 **Website:** http://www.qwest.com	**JOHNSON CONTROLS** **CEO:** James H. Keyes **Address:** 5757 N. Green Bay Ave. Milwaukee, WI 53201 **Phone:** 414-524-1200 **Website:** http://www.johnsoncontrols.com
VIACOM **CEO:** Sumner M. Redstone **Address:** 1515 Broadway New York, NY 10036 **Phone:** 212-258-6000 **Website:** http://www.viacom.com	**LOWE S** **CEO:** Robert L. Tillman **Address:** 1605 Curtis Bridge Rd. Wilkesboro, NC 28697 **Phone:** 336-658-4000 **Website:** http://www.lowes.com	**FEDEX** **CEO:** Frederick W. Smith **Address:** 942 S. Shady Grove Rd. Memphis, TN 38120 **Phone:** 901-818-7500 **Website:** http://www.fedex.com	**SUN MICROSYSTEMS** **CEO:** Scott G. McNealy **Address:** 901 San Antonio Rd. Palo Alto, CA 94303 **Phone:** 650-960-1300 **Website:** http://www.sun.com
SUPERVALU **CEO:** Jeffrey Noddle **Address:** 11840 Valley View Rd. Eden Prairie, MN 55344 **Phone:** 952-828-4000 **Website:** http://www.supervalu.com	**SYSCO** **CEO:** Charles H. Cotros **Address:** 1390 Enclave Pkwy. Houston, TX 77077 **Phone:** 281-584-1390 **Website:** http://www.sysco.com	Mass. Mutual Life Insurance **CEO:** Robert J. O'Connell **Address:** 1295 State St. Springfield, MA 01111 **Phone:** 413-788-8411 **Website:** http://www.massmutual.com	**HCA** **CEO:** Jack O. Bovender Jr. **Address:** 1 Park Plaza Nashville, TN 37203 **Phone:** 615-344-9551 **Website:** http://www.hcahealthcare.com
PG&E CORP. **CEO:** Robert D. Glynn Jr. **Address:** 1 Market St. San Francisco, CA 94105 **Phone:** 415-267-7000 **Website:** http://www.pgecorp.com	Bristol-Myers Squibb **CEO:** Peter R. Dolan **Address:** 345 Park Ave. New York, NY 10154 **Phone:** 212-546-4000 **Website:** http://www.bms.com	**PHARMACIA** **CEO:** Fred Hassan **Address:** 100 Route 206 N. Peapack, NJ 07977 **Phone:** 908-901-8000 **Website:** http://www.pharmacia.com	**VISTEON** **CEO:** Peter J. Pestillo **Address:** 5500 Auto Club Dr. Dearborn, MI 48126 **Phone:** 313-755-2800 **Website:** http://www.visteon.com
ALCOA **CEO:** Alain J.P. Belda **Address:** 201 Isabella St. Pittsburgh, PA 15212 **Phone:** 412-553-4545 **Website:** http://www.alcoa.com	Electronic Data Systems **CEO:** Richard H. Brown **Address:** 5400 Legacy Dr. Plano, TX 75024 **Phone:** 972-604-6000 **Website:** http://www.eds.com	**FLEETBOSTON** **CEO:** Charles K. Gifford **Address:** 100 Federal St. Boston, MA 02110 **Phone:** 617-434-2200 **Website:** http://www.fleet.com	**SARA LEE** **CEO:** C. Steven McMillan **Address:** 3 First National Plaza Chicago, IL 60602 **Phone:** 312-726-2600 **Website:** http://www.saralee.com
AMERICAN EXPRESS **CEO:** Kenneth I. Chenault **Address:** 200 Vesey St. New York, NY 10285 **Phone:** 212-640-2000 **Website:** http://www.americanexpress.com	**CATERPILLAR** **CEO:** Glen A. Barton **Address:** 100 N.E. Adams St. Peoria, IL 61629 **Phone:** 309-675-1000 **Website:** http://www.cat.com	**CIGNA** **CEO:** H. Edward Hanway **Address:** 1 Liberty Place Philadelphia, PA 19192 **Phone:** 215-761-1000 **Website:** http://www.cigna.com	**WASHINGTON MUTUAL** **CEO:** Kerry K. Killinger **Address:** 1201 Third Ave. Seattle, WA 98101 **Phone:** 206-461-2000 **Website:** http://www.wamu.com
WACHOVIA CORP. **CEO:** G. Kennedy Thompson **Address:** 301 S College St. Charlotte, NC 28288 **Phone:** 704-374-6161 **Website:** http://www.wachovia.com	COCA-COLA **CEO:** Douglas N. Daft **Address:** 1 Coca-Cola Plaza Atlanta, GA 30313 **Phone:** 404-676-2121 **Website:** http://www.coca-cola.com	**AMR** **CEO:** Donald J. Carty **Address:** 4333 Amon Carter Blvd. Fort Worth, TX 76155 **Phone:** 817-963-1234 **Website:** http://www.amrcorp.com	**TECH DATA** **CEO:** Steven A. Raymund **Address:** 5350 Tech Data Dr. Clearwater, FL 33760 **Phone:** 727-539-7429 **Website:** http://www.techdata.com
LEHMAN BROTHERS HOLDINGS **CEO:** Richard S. Fuld Jr. **Address:** 745 Seventh Avenue New York, NY 10019 **Phone:** 212-526-7000 **Website:** http://www.lehman.com	Archer Daniels Midland **CEO:** G. Allen Andreas **Address:** 4666 Faries Pkwy. Decatur, IL 62525 **Phone:** 217-424-5200 **Website:** http://www.admworld.com	LOEWS **CEO:** James S. Tisch **Address:** 667 Madison Ave. New York, NY 10021 **Phone:** 212-521-2000 **Website:** http://www.loews.com	FEDERATED DEPT. STORES **CEO:** James M. Zimmerman **Address:** 7 W. Seventh St. Cincinnati, OH 45202 **Phone:** 513-579-7000 **Website:** http://www.federated-fds.com
CISCO SYSTEMS **CEO:** John T. Chambers **Address:** 170 W. Tasman Dr. San Jose, CA 95134 **Phone:** 408-526-4000 **Website:** http://www.cisco.com	**SOLECTRON** **CEO:** Michael J. Jackson **Address:** 110 S.E. Sixth St. Fort Lauderdale, FL 33301 **Phone:** 954-769-6000 **Website:** http://www.autonation.com	**SOLECTRON** **CEO:** Koichi Nishimura **Address:** 777 Gibraltar Dr. Milpitas, CA 95035 **Phone:** 408-957-8500 **Website:** http://www.solectron.com	**RAYTHEON** **CEO:** Daniel P. Burnham **Address:** 141 Spring St. Lexington, MA 02421 **Phone:** 781-862-6600 **Website:** http://www.raytheon.com

XEROX	FLEMING	VALERO ENERGY	Household international
CEO: Anne Mulcahy	**CEO:** Mark Hansen	**CEO:** William E. Greehey	**CEO:** William F. Aldinger III
Address:	**Address:**	**Address:**	**Address:**
800 Long Ridge Rd.	1945 Lakepointe Dr.	1 Valero Place	2700 Sanders Rd.
Stamford, CT 06904	Lewisville, TX 75057	San Antonio, TX 78212	Prospect Heights, IL 60070
Phone:	**Phone:**	**Phone:**	**Phone:**
203-968-3000	972-906-8000	210-370-2000	847-564-5000
Website:	**Website:**	**Website:**	**Website:**
http://www.xerox.com	http://www.fleming.com	http://www.valero.com	http://www.household.com
U.S. BANCORP.	EMERSON ELECTRIC	MCDONALD S	Delta air lines
CEO: Jerry A. Grundhofer	**CEO:** David N. Farr	**CEO:** Jack M. Greenberg	**CEO:** Leo F. Mullin
Address:	**Address:**	**Address:**	**Address:**
601 Second Ave. S.	8000 W. Florissant Ave.	One Kroc Dr.	1030 Delta Blvd.
Minneapolis, MN 55402	St. Louis, MO 63136	Oak Brook, IL 60523	Atlanta, GA 30320
Phone:	**Phone:**	**Phone:**	**Phone:**
612-973-1111	314-553-2000	630-623-3000	404-715-2600
Website:	**Website:**	**Website:**	**Website:**
http://www.usbank.com	http://www.gotoemerson.com	http://www.mcdonalds.com	http://www.delta.com
TRW	BEST BUY	Weyerhaeuser	Gap
CEO: Philip A. Odeen	**CEO:** Richard M. Schulze	**CEO:** Steven R. Rogel	**CEO:** Millard S. Drexler
Address:	**Address:**	**Address:**	**Address:**
1900 Richmond Rd.	7075 Flying Cloud Dr.	33663 Weyerhaeuser Way S.	2 Folsom Street
Cleveland, OH 44124	Eden Prairie, MN 55344	Federal Way, WA 98063	San Francisco, CA 94105
Phone:	**Phone:**	**Phone:**	**Phone:**
216-291-7000	952-947-2000	253-924-2345	650-952-4400
Website:	**Website:**	**Website:**	**Website:**
http://www.trw.com	http://www.bestbuy.com	http://www.weyerhaeuser.com	http://www.gap.com
Abbott Laboratories	RITE AID	KIMBERLY-CLARK	Lear
CEO: Miles D. White	**CEO:** Robert G. Miller	**CEO:** Wayne R. Sanders	**CEO:** Robert E. Rossiter
Address:	**Address:**	**Address:**	**Address:**
100 Abbott Park Rd.	30 Hunter Lane	351 Phelps Dr.	21557 Telegraph Rd.
Abbott Park, IL 60064	Camp Hill, PA 17011	Irving, TX 75038	Southfield, MI 48034
Phone:	**Phone:**	**Phone:**	**Phone:**
847-937-6100	717-761-2633	972-281-1200	248-447-1500
Website:	**Website:**	**Website:**	**Website:**
http://www.abbott.com	http://www.riteaid.com	http://www.kimberly-clark.com	http://www.lear.com
NORTHWESTERN MUTUAL	PUBLIX	Liberty Mutual Insurance Group	Northrop Grumman
CEO: Edward J. Zore	**CEO:** Charles H. Jenkins Jr.	**CEO:** Edmund F. Kelly	**CEO:** Kent Kresa
Address:	**Address:**	**Address:**	**Address:**
720 E. Wisconsin Ave.	1936 George Jenkins Blvd.	175 Berkeley St.	1840 Century Park E.
Milwaukee, WI 53202	Lakeland, FL 33815	Boston, MA 02117	Los Angeles, CA 90067
Phone:	**Phone:**	**Phone:**	**Phone:**
414-271-1444	863-688-1188	617-357-9500	310-553-6262
Website:	**Website:**	**Website:**	**Website:**
http://www.northwesternmutual.com	http://www.publix.com	http://www.libertymutual.com	http://www.northropgrumman.
UAL	HARTFORD FIN. SERV.	May Department Stores	AMERADA HESS
CEO: John W. Creighton Jr.	**CEO:** Ramani Ayer	**CEO:** Eugene S. Kahn	**CEO:** John B. Hess
Address:	**Address:**	**Address:**	**Address:**
1200 E. Algonquin Rd.	690 Asylum Avenue	611 Olive St.	1185 Sixth Ave
Elk Grove Tnshp., IL 60007	Hartford, CT 06115	St. Louis, MO 63101	New York, NY 10036
Phone:	**Phone:**	**Phone:**	**Phone:**
847-700-4000	860-547-5000	314-342-6300	212-997-8500
Website:	**Website:**	**Website:**	**Website:**
http://www.united.com	http://www.thehartford.com	http://www.maycompany.com	http://www.hess.com
Minnesota Mining & Mfg.	EXELON	GOODYEAR TIRE	CMS ENERGY
CEO: W. James McNerney Jr.	**CEO:** John W. Rowe	**CEO:** Samir G. Gibara	**CEO:** William T. McCormick Jr.
Address:	**Address:**	**Address:**	**Address:**
3M Center	10 S. Dearborn St.	1144 E. Market St.	330 Town Center Dr.
St. Paul, MN 55144	Chicago, IL 60680	Akron, OH 44316	Dearborn, MI 48126
Phone:	**Phone:**	**Phone:**	**Phone:**
651-733-1110	312-394-7398	330-796-2121	313-436-9200
Website:	**Website:**	**Website:**	**Website:**
http://www.3m.com	http://www.exeloncorp.com	http://www.goodyear.com	http://www.cmsenergy.com
AmerisourceBergen	NATIONWIDE	WYETH	CIRCUIT CITY STORES
CEO: R. David Yost	**CEO:** William G. Jurgenson	**CEO:** Robert A. Essner	**CEO:** W. Alan McCollough
Address:	**Address:**	**Address:**	**Address:**
1300 Morris Dr.	1 Nationwide Plaza	5 Giralda Farms	9950 Mayland Dr.
Chesterbrook, PA 19087	Columbus, OH 43215	Madison, NJ 07940	Richmond, VA 23233
Phone:	**Phone:**	**Phone:**	**Phone:**
610-727-7000	614-249-7111	973-660-5000	804-527-4000
Website:	**Website:**	**Website:**	**Website:**
http://www.amerisourcebergen	http://www.nationwide.com	http://www.wyeth.com	http://www.circuitcity.com
Coca-Cola Enterprises	XCEL ENERGY	Occidental Petroleum	CINERGY
CEO: Lowry F. Kline	**CEO:** Wayne Brunetti	**CEO:** Ray R. Irani	**CEO:** James E. Rogers
Address:	**Address:**	**Address:**	**Address:**
2500 Windy Ridge Pkwy.	800 Nicollet Mall	10889 Wilshire Blvd.	139 E. Fourth St.
Atlanta, GA 30339	Minneapolis, MN 55402	Los Angeles, CA 90024	Cincinnati, OH 45202
Phone:	**Phone:**	**Phone:**	**Phone:**
770-989-3000	612-330-5500	310-208-8800	513-421-9500
Website:	**Website:**	**Website:**	**Website:**
http://www.cokecce.com	http://www.xcelenergy.com	http://www.oxy.com	http://www.cinergy.com

ANHEUSER-BUSCH **CEO:** August A. Busch III **Address:** 1 Busch Place St. Louis, MO 63118 **Phone:** 314-577-2000 **Website:** http://www.anheuser-busch.com	**UNION PACIFIC** **CEO:** Richard K. Davidson **Address:** 1416 Dodge St. Omaha, NE 68179 **Phone:** 402-271-5777 **Website:** http://www.up.com	**TYSON FOODS** **CEO:** John H. Tyson **Address:** 2210 W. Oaklawn Dr. Springdale, AR 72762 **Phone:** 501-290-4000 **Website:** http://www.tyson.com	**WHIRLPOOL** **CEO:** David R. Whitwam **Address:** 2000 North M-63 Benton Harbor, MI 49022 **Phone:** 616-923-5000 **Website:** http://www.whirlpoolcorp.com
WINN DIXIE STORES **CEO:** Allen R. Rowland **Address:** 5050 Edgewood Court Jacksonville, FL 32254 **Phone:** 904-783-5000 **Website:** http://www.winn-dixie.com	**PACIFICARE HEALTH SYSTEMS** **CEO:** Howard G. Phanstiel **Address:** 3120 W. Lake Center Dr. Santa Ana, CA 92704 **Phone:** 714-825-5200 **Website:** http://www.pacificare.com	**STAPLES** **CEO:** Ronald L. Sargent **Address:** 500 Staples Dr. Framingham, MA 01702 **Phone:** 508-253-5000 **Website:** http://www.staples.com	**HUMANA** **CEO:** Michael B. McCallister **Address:** 500 W. Main St. Louisville, KY 40202 **Phone:** 502-580-1000 **Website:** http://www.humana.com
AVNET **CEO:** Roy Vallee **Address:** 2211 S. 47th St. Phoenix, AZ 85034 **Phone:** 480-643-2000 **Website:** http://www.avnet.com	**FARMLAND INDUSTRIES** **CEO:** Robert W. Honse **Address:** 12200 N. Ambassador Dr. Kansas City, MO 64163 **Phone:** 816-713-7000 **Website:** http://www.farmland.com	**TJX** **CEO:** Edmond J. English **Address:** 770 Cochituate Rd. Framingham, MA 01701 **Phone:** 508-390-1000 **Website:** http://www.tjx.com	**SOUTHERN** **CEO:** H. Allen Franklin **Address:** 270 Peachtree St. N.W. Atlanta, GA 30303 **Phone:** 404-506-5000 **Website:** http://www.southernco.com
WellPoint Health Networks **CEO:** Leonard D. Schaeffer **Address:** 1 WellPoint Way Thousand Oaks, CA 91362 **Phone:** 805-557-6655 **Website:** http://www.wellpoint.com	**ELI LILLY** **CEO:** Sidney Taurel **Address:** 893 S. Delaware St. Indianapolis, IN 46285 **Phone:** 317-276-2000 **Website:** http://www.lilly.com	**DOMINION RESOURCES** **CEO:** Thomas E. Capps **Address:** 120 Tredegar St. Richmond, VA 23219 **Phone:** 804-819-2000 **Website:** http://www.dom.com	**MARRIOTT INTERNATIONAL** **CEO:** J. Willard Marriott Jr. **Address:** 10400 Fernwood Rd. Bethesda, MD 20817 **Phone:** 301-380-3000 **Website:** http://www.marriott.com
SUNOCO **CEO:** John G. Drosdick **Address:** 1801 Market St. Philadelphia, PA 19103 **Phone:** 215-977-3000 **Website:** http://www.sunocoinc.com	**WASTE MANAGEMENT** **CEO:** A. Maurice Myers **Address:** 1001 Fannin St. Houston, TX 77002 **Phone:** 713-512-6200 **Website:** http://www.wm.com	**COMPUTER SCIENCES** **CEO:** Van B. Honeycutt **Address:** 2100 E. Grand Ave. El Segundo, CA 90245 **Phone:** 310-615-0311 **Website:** http://www.csc.com	**MBNA** **CEO:** Alfred Lerner **Address:** 1100 N. King St. Wilmington, DE 19884 **Phone:** 800-441-7048 **Website:** http://www.mbna.com
TEXTRON **CEO:** Lewis B. Campbell **Address:** 40 Westminster St. Providence, RI 02903 **Phone:** 401-421-2800 **Website:** http://www.textron.com	**OFFICE DEPOT** **CEO:** M. Bruce Nelson **Address:** 2200 Old Germantown Rd. Delray Beach, FL 33445 **Phone:** 561-438-4800 **Website:** http://www.officedepot.com	**MANPOWER** **CEO:** Jeffrey A. Joerres **Address:** 5301 N. Ironwood Rd. Milwaukee, WI 53217 **Phone:** 414-961-1000 **Website:** http://www.manpower.com	**ARROW ELCTRONICS** **CEO:** Francis M. Scricco **Address:** 25 Hub Dr. Melville, NY 11747 **Phone:** 631-391-1300 **Website:** http://www.arrow.com
EDISON INTERNATIONAL **CEO:** John E. Bryson **Address:** 2244 Walnut Grove Ave. Rosemead, CA 91770 **Phone:** 626-302-1212 **Website:** http://www.edison.com	**WILLIAMS** **CEO:** Steven J. Malcolm **Address:** 1 Williams Center Tulsa, OK 74172 **Phone:** 918-573-2000 **Website:** http://www.williams.com	**DANA** **CEO:** Joseph Magliochetti **Address:** 4500 Dorr St. Toledo, OH 43615 **Phone:** 419-535-4500 **Website:** http://www.dana.com	**HEALTH NET** **CEO:** Jay M. Gellert **Address:** 21650 Oxnard St. Woodland Hills, CA 91367 **Phone:** 818-676-6000 **Website:** http://www.health.net
GENERAL DYNAMICS **CEO:** Nicholas D. Chabraja **Address:** 3190 Fairview Park Dr. Falls Church, VA 22042 **Phone:** 703-876-3000 **Website:** http://www.gd.com	**TOYS R US** **CEO:** John H. Eyler Jr. **Address:** 461 From Rd. Paramus, NJ 07652 **Phone:** 201-262-7800 **Website:** http://www.toysrus.com	**ANTHEM** **CEO:** Larry Glasscock **Address:** 120 Monument Circle Indianapolis, IN 46204 **Phone:** 317-488-6000 **Website:** http://www.anthem.com	**Marsh & McLennan** **CEO:** Jeffrey W. Greenberg **Address:** 1166 Sixth Ave. New York, NY 10036 **Phone:** 212-345-5000 **Website:** http://www.mmc.com
TENET HEALTHCARE **CEO:** Jeffrey C. Barbakow **Address:** 3820 State St. Santa Barbara, CA 93105 **Phone:** 805-563-7000 **Website:** http://www.tenethealth.com	**ORACLE** **CEO:** Lawrence J. Ellison **Address:** 500 Oracle Pkwy. Redwood City, CA 94065 **Phone:** 650-506-7000 **Website:** http://www.oracle.com	**ALLEGHENY ENERGY** **CEO:** Alan J. Noia **Address:** 10435 Downsville Pike Hagerstown, MD 21740 **Phone:** 301-790-3400 **Website:** http://www.alleghenyenergy.com	**NORTHWEST AIRLINES** **CEO:** Richard H. Anderson **Address:** 2700 Lone Oak Pkwy. Eagan, MN 55121 **Phone:** 612-726-2111 **Website:** http://www.nwa.com

Public Service Enterprise Group **CEO:** E. James Ferland **Address:** 80 Park Plaza Newark, NJ 07101 **Phone:** 973-430-7000 **Website:** http://www.pseg.com	**NIKE** **CEO:** Philip H. Knight **Address:** 1 Bowerman Dr. Beaverton, OR 97005 **Phone:** 503-671-6453 **Website:** http://www.nike.com	**PRINCIPAL FINANCIAL** **CEO:** J. Barry Griswell **Address:** 711 High St. Des Moines, IA 50392 **Phone:** 515-247-5111 **Website:** http://www.principal.com	**CSX** **CEO:** John W. Snow **Address:** 901 E. Cary St. Richmond, VA 23219 **Phone:** 804-782-1400 **Website:** http://www.csx.com
Schering-Plough **CEO:** Richard Jay Kogan **Address:** 2000 Galloping Hill Rd. Kenilworth, NJ 07033 **Phone:** 908-298-4000 **Website:** http://www.schering-plough.com	**UnumProvident** **CEO:** J. Harold Chandler **Address:** 1 Fountain Square Chattanooga, TN 37402 **Phone:** 423-755-1011 **Website:** http://www.unum.com	**SCI SYSTEMS** **CEO:** Jure Sola **Address:** 2101 W. Clinton Ave. Huntsville, AL 35805 **Phone:** 256-882-4800 **Website:** http://www.sci.com	**CONSECO** **CEO:** Gary C. Wendt **Address:** 11825 N. Pennsylvania St. Carmel, IN 46032 **Phone:** 317-817-6100 **Website:** http://www.conseco.com
Illinois Tool Works **CEO:** W. James Farrell **Address:** 3600 W. Lake Ave. Glenview, IL 60025 **Phone:** 847-724-7500 **Website:** http://www.itw.com	**H.J. Heinz** **CEO:** William R. Johnson **Address:** 600 Grant St. Pittsburgh, PA 15219 **Phone:** 412-456-5700 **Website:** http://www.heinz.com	**BEAR STEARNS** **CEO:** James E. Cayne **Address:** 383 Madison Ave. New York, NY 10179 **Phone:** 212-272-2000 **Website:** http://www.bearstearns.com	**GILLETTE** **CEO:** James M. Kilts **Address:** Prudential Tower Building Boston, MA 02199 **Phone:** 617-421-7000 **Website:** http://www.gillette.com
COMCAST **CEO:** Brian L. Roberts **Address:** 1500 Market St. Philadelphia, PA 19102 **Phone:** 215-665-1700 **Website:** http://www.comcast.com	**Colgate-Palmolive** **CEO:** Reuben Mark **Address:** 300 Park Ave. New York, NY 10022 **Phone:** 212-310-2000 **Website:** http://www.colgate.com	**R.J. Reynolds Tobacco** **CEO:** Andrew J. Schindler **Address:** 401 N. Main St. Winston-Salem, NC 27102 **Phone:** 336-741-5500 **Website:** http://www.rjrt.com	**SEMPRA ENERGY** **CEO:** Stephen L. Baum **Address:** 101 Ash St. San Diego, CA 92101 **Phone:** 619-696-2000 **Website:** http://www.sempra.com
CONSOLIDATED EDISON **CEO:** Eugene R. McGrath **Address:** 4 Irving Place New York, NY 10003 **Phone:** 212-460-4600 **Website:** http://www.conedison.com	**LIMITED** **CEO:** Leslie H. Wexner **Address:** 3 Limited Pkwy. Columbus, OH 43230 **Phone:** 614-415-7000 **Website:** http://www.limited.com	**ASHLAND** **CEO:** Paul W. Chellgren **Address:** 50 E. RiverCenter Blvd. Covington, KY 41012 **Phone:** 859-815-3333 **Website:** http://www.ashland.com	**FIRSTENERGY** **CEO:** H. Peter Burg **Address:** 76 S. Main St. Akron, OH 44308 **Phone:** 800-646-0400 **Website:** http://www.firstenergycorp.com
ENTERGY **CEO:** J. Wayne Leonard **Address:** 639 Loyola Ave. New Orleans, LA 70113 **Phone:** 504-576-4000 **Website:** http://www.entergy.com	**John Hancock Financial Services** **CEO:** David F. O'Alessandro **Address:** John Hancock Place Boston, MA 02117 **Phone:** 617-572-6000 **Website:** http://www.jhancock.com	**FPL GROUP** **CEO:** Lewis Hay III **Address:** 700 Universe Blvd. Juno Beach, FL 33408 **Phone:** 561-694-4000 **Website:** http://www.fplgroup.com	**CLEAR CHANNEL COMMUNICATIONS** **CEO:** L. Lowry Mays **Address:** 200 East Basse Road San Antonio, TX 78209 **Phone:** 210-822-2828 **Website:** http://www.clearchannel.com
AES **CEO:** Dennis W. Bakke **Address:** 1001 N. 19th St. Arlington, VA 22209 **Phone:** 703-522-1315 **Website:** http://www.aesc.com	**Express Scripts** **CEO:** Barrett A. Toan **Address:** 13900 Riverport Dr. Maryland Heights, MO 63043 **Phone:** 314-770-1666 **Website:** http://www.express-scripts.com	**PROGRESS ENERGY** **CEO:** William Cavanaugh III **Address:** 410 S. Wilmington St. Raleigh, NC 27601 **Phone:** 919-546-6111 **Website:** http://www.progress-energy.com	**CENEX HARVEST STATES** **CEO:** John D. Johnson **Address:** 5500 Cenex Dr. Inver Grove Heights, MN 55077 **Phone:** 651-451-5151 **Website:** http://www.chsco-ops.com
AFLAC **CEO:** Daniel P. Amos **Address:** 1932 Wynnton Rd. Columbus, GA 31999 **Phone:** 706-323-3431 **Website:** http://www.aflac.com	**Burlington Northern Santa Fe** **CEO:** Matthew K. Rose **Address:** 2500 Lou Menk Dr. Fort Worth, TX 76131 **Phone:** 817-333-2000 **Website:** http://www.bnsf.com	**PEPSI BOTTLING** **CEO:** John T. Cahill **Address:** 1 Pepsi Way Somers, NY 10589 **Phone:** 914-767-6000 **Website:** http://www.pbg.com	**DTE ENERGY** **CEO:** Anthony F. Earley Jr. **Address:** 2000 Second Ave. Detroit, MI 48226 **Phone:** 313-235-4000 **Website:** http://www.dteenergy.com
NISOURCE **CEO:** Gary L. Neale **Address:** 801 E. 86th Ave. Merrillville, IN 46410 **Phone:** 877-647-5990 **Website:** http://www.nisource.com	**Agilent Technologies** **CEO:** Edward W. Barnholt **Address:** 395 Page Mill Rd. Palo Alto, CA 94306 **Phone:** 650-752-5000 **Website:** http://www.agilent.com	**SUNTRUST BANKS** **CEO:** L. Phillip Humann **Address:** 303 Peachtree St. N.E. Atlanta, GA 30308 **Phone:** 404-588-7711 **Website:** http://www.suntrust.com	**ARAMARK** **CEO:** Joseph Neubauer **Address:** 1101 Market St. Philadelphia, PA 19107 **Phone:** 215-238-3000 **Website:** http://www.aramark.com

NATIONAL CITY CORP. **CEO:** David A. Daberko **Address:** 1900 E. Ninth St. Cleveland, OH 44114 **Phone:** 216-575-2000 **Website:** http://www.nationalcity.com	**Smurfit-Stone Container** **CEO:** Patrick J. Moore **Address:** 150 N. Michigan Ave. Chicago, IL 60601 **Phone:** 312-346-6600 **Website:** http://www.smurfit-stone.net	**CHUBB** **CEO:** Dean R. O'Hare **Address:** 15 Mountain View Rd. Warren, NJ 07061 **Phone:** 908-903-2000 **Website:** http://www.chubb.com	**GENERAL MILLS** **CEO:** Stephen W. Sanger **Address:** 1 General Mills Blvd. Minneapolis, MN 55426 **Phone:** 763-764-7600 **Website:** http://www.generalmills.com
FLUOR **CEO:** Alan L. Boeckmann **Address:** 1 Enterprise Dr. Aliso Viejo, CA 92656 **Phone:** 949-349-2000 **Website:** http://www.fluor.com	**Anadarko Petroleum** **CEO:** John N. Seitz **Address:** 1201 Lake Robbins Dr. The Woodlands, TX 77380 **Phone:** 832-636-1000 **Website:** http://www.anadarko.com	**ALLTEL** **CEO:** Joe T. Ford **Address:** 1 Allied Dr. Little Rock, AR 72202 **Phone:** 501-905-8000 **Website:** http://www.alltel.com	**ADVANCE PCS** **CEO:** David D. Halbert **Address:** 5215 N. O'Connor Blvd. Irving, TX 75039 **Phone:** 469-420-6000 **Website:** http://www.advparadigm.com
USAA **CEO:** Robert G. Davis **Address:** 9800 Fredericksburg Rd. San Antonio, TX 78288 **Phone:** 210-498-2211 **Website:** http://www.usaa.com	**MASCO** **CEO:** Richard A. Manoogian **Address:** 21001 Van Born Rd. Taylor, MI 48180 **Phone:** 313-274-7400 **Website:** http://www.masco.com	**CALPINE** **CEO:** Peter Cartwright **Address:** 50 W. San Fernando St. San Jose, CA 95113 **Phone:** 408-995-5115 **Website:** http://www.calpine.com	**AUTOMATIC DATA PROCESSING** **CEO:** Arthur F. Weinbach **Address:** 1 ADP Blvd. Roseland, NJ 07068 **Phone:** 973-974-5000 **Website:** http://www.adp.com
CONTINENTAL AIRLINES **CEO:** Gordon M. Bethune **Address:** 1600 Smith St. Houston, TX 77002 **Phone:** 713-324-5000 **Website:** http://www.continental.com	**US AIRWAYS GROUP** **CEO:** David N. Siegel **Address:** 2345 Crystal Dr. Arlington, VA 22227 **Phone:** 703-872-5100 **Website:** http://www.usairways.com	**NEXTEL COMMUNICATIONS** **CEO:** Tim M. Donahue **Address:** 2001 Edmund Halley Dr. Reston, VA 20191 **Phone:** 703-433-4000 **Website:** http://www.nextel.com	**SAFECO** **CEO:** Mike McGavick **Address:** 4333 Brooklyn Ave., N.E. Seattle, WA 98185 **Phone:** 206-545-5000 **Website:** http://www.safeco.com
CENDANT **CEO:** Henry R. Silverman **Address:** 9 W. 57th Street New York, NY 10019 **Phone:** 212-413-1800 **Website:** http://www.cendant.com	**GENUINE PARTS** **CEO:** Larry L. Prince **Address:** 2999 Circle 75 Pkwy. Atlanta, GA 30339 **Phone:** 770-953-1700 **Website:** http://www.genpt.com	**KOHL S** **CEO:** R. Lawrence Montgomery **Address:** N56 W. 17000 Ridgewood Dr. Menomonee Falls, WI 53051 **Phone:** 262-703-7000 **Website:** http://www.kohls.com	**Tricon Global Restaurants** **CEO:** David C. Novak **Address:** 1441 Gardiner Lane Louisville, KY 40213 **Phone:** 502-874-8300 **Website:** http://www.triconglobal.com
ST. PAUL COS. **CEO:** Jay S. Fishman **Address:** 385 Washington St. St. Paul, MN 55102 **Phone:** 651-310-7911 **Website:** http://www.stpaul.com	**TEXAS INSTRUMENTS** **CEO:** Thomas J. Engibous **Address:** 12500 TI Blvd. Dallas, TX 75266 **Phone:** 972-995-6611 **Website:** http://www.ti.com	**PROGRESSIVE** **CEO:** Glenn M. Renwick **Address:** 6300 Wilson Mills Rd. Mayfield Village, OH 44143 **Phone:** 440-461-5000 **Website:** http://www.progressive.com	**PNC Financial Services Group** **CEO:** James E. Rohr **Address:** 249 Fifth Ave. Pittsburgh, PA 15222 **Phone:** 412-762-2000 **Website:** http://www.pnc.com
Guardian Life Ins. Co. of America **CEO:** Joseph D. Sargent **Address:** 7 Hanover Square New York, NY 10004 **Phone:** 212-598-8000 **Website:** http://www.glic.com	**PPG INDUSTRIES** **CEO:** Raymond W. LeBoeuf **Address:** 1 PPG Place Pittsburgh, PA 15272 **Phone:** 412-434-3131 **Website:** http://www.ppg.com	**AMERICAN STANDARD** **CEO:** Frederic M. Poses **Address:** 1 Centennial Ave. Piscataway, NJ 08855 **Phone:** 732-980-6000 **Website:** http://www.americanstandard.COM	**Newell Rubbermaid** **CEO:** Joseph Galli Jr. **Address:** 29 E. Stephenson St. Freeport, IL 61032 **Phone:** 815-235-4171 **Website:** http://www.newellco.com
KELLOGG **CEO:** Carlos M. Gutierrez **Address:** 1 Kellogg Square Battle Creek, MI 49016 **Phone:** 616-961-2000 **Website:** http://www.kelloggs.com	**AON** **CEO:** Patrick G. Ryan **Address:** 200 E. Randolph St. Chicago, IL 60601 **Phone:** 312-381-1000 **Website:** http://www.aon.com	**BOISE CSCADE** **CEO:** George J. Harad **Address:** 1111 W. Jefferson St. Boise, ID 83702 **Phone:** 208-384-6161 **Website:** http://www.bc.com	**KEY SPAN** **CEO:** Robert B. Catell **Address:** 1 MetroTech Center Brooklyn, NY 11201 **Phone:** 718-403-2000 **Website:** http://www.keyspanenergy.com
DILLARD S **CEO:** William Dillard II **Address:** 1600 Cantrell Rd. Little Rock, AR 72201 **Phone:** 501-376-5200 **Website:** http://www.dillards.com	**BAXTER INTERNATIONAL** **CEO:** Harry M. Jansen Kraemer Jr. **Address:** 1 Baxter Pkwy. Deerfield, IL 60015 **Phone:** 847-948-2000 **Website:** http://www.baxter.com	**KEY CORP.** **CEO:** Henry L. Meyer III **Address:** 127 Public Square Cleveland, OH 44114 **Phone:** 216-689-6300 **Website:** http://www.keybank.com	**OMNICOM GROUP** **CEO:** John D. Wren **Address:** 437 Madison Ave. New York, NY 10022 **Phone:** 212-415-3600 **Website:** http://www.omnicomgroup.com

NORTHEAST UTILITIES **CEO:** Michael G. Morris **Address:** 107 Selden St. Berlin, CT 06037 **Phone:** 860-665-5000 **Website:** http://www.nu.com	**CAMPBELL SOUP** **CEO:** Douglas R. Conant **Address:** Campbell Place Camden, NJ 08103 **Phone:** 856-342-4800 **Website:** http://www.campbellsoup.com	**BB&T CORP.** **CEO:** John A. Allison IV **Address:** 200 W. Second St. Winston-Salem, NC 27101 **Phone:** 336-733-2000 **Website:** http://www.bbandt.com	**UNISYS** **CEO:** Lawrence A. Weinbach **Address:** Unisys Way Blue Bell, PA 19424 **Phone:** 215-986-4011 **Website:** http://www.unisys.com
Plains All American Pipeline **CEO:** Greg L. Armstrong **Address:** 333 Clay St. Houston, TX 77002 **Phone:** 713-646-4100 **Website:** http://www.paalp.com	**FIFTH THIRD BANCORP.** **CEO:** George A. Schaefer Jr. **Address:** 38 Fountain Square Plaza Cincinnati, OH 45263 **Phone:** 513-579-5300 **Website:** http://www.53.com	**UNITED AUTO GROUP** **CEO:** Roger S. Penske **Address:** 13400 Outer Drive W. Detroit, MI 48239 **Phone:** 313-592-7311 **Website:** http://www.unitedauto.com	**Owens-Illinois** **CEO:** Joseph H. Lemieux **Address:** 1 SeaGate Toledo, OH 43666 **Phone:** 419-247-5000 **Website:** http://www.o-i.com
ArvinMeritor **CEO:** Larry D. Yost **Address:** 2135 W. Maple Rd. Troy, MI 48084 **Phone:** 248-435-1000 **Website:** http://www.arvinmeritor.com	**FIRST DATE** **CEO:** Charles T. Fote **Address:** 6200 S. Quebec St. Greenwood Village, CO 80111 **Phone:** 303-488-8000 **Website:** http://www.firstdata.com	**NORFOLK SOUTHERN** **CEO:** David R. Goode **Address:** 3 Commercial Place Norfolk, VA 23510 **Phone:** 757-629-2600 **Website:** http://www.nscorp.com	**AVON PRODUCTS** **CEO:** Andrea Jung **Address:** 1345 Sixth Ave. New York, NY 10105 **Phone:** 212-282-5000 **Website:** http://www.avon.com
ONEOK **CEO:** David Kyle **Address:** 100 W. Fifth St. Tulsa, OK 74103 **Phone:** 918-588-7000 **Website:** http://www.oneok.com	**PRMCOR** **CEO:** Thomas D. O'Malley **Address:** 8182 Maryland Ave. St. Louis, MO 63105 **Phone:** 314-854-9696 **Website:** http://www.premcor.com	**SCIENCE APPLICATIONS INTERNATIONAL** **CEO:** J. Robert Beyster **Address:** 10260 Campus Point Dr San Diego, CA 92121 **Phone:** 858-826-6000 **Website:** http://www.saic.com	**PARKER HANNIFIN** **CEO:** Donald E. Washkewicz **Address:** 6035 Parkland Blvd. Cleveland, OH 44124 **Phone:** 216-896-3000 **Website:** http://www.parker.com
AVAYA **CEO:** Donald K. Peterson **Address:** 211 Mount Airy Rd. Basking Ridge, NJ 07920 **Phone:** 908-953-6000 **Website:** http://www.avaya.com	**LINCOLN NATIONAL** **CEO:** Jon A. Boscia **Address:** 1500 Market St. Philadelphia, PA 19102 **Phone:** 215-448-1400 **Website:** http://www.lfg.com	**PACCAR** **CEO:** Mark C. Pigott **Address:** 777 106th Ave. N.E. Bellevue, WA 98004 **Phone:** 425-468-7400 **Website:** http://www.paccar.com	**NCR** **CEO:** Lars Nyberg **Address:** 1700 S. Patterson Blvd. Dayton, OH 45479 **Phone:** 937-445-5000 **Website:** http://www.ncr.com
UNOCAL **CEO:** Charles R. Williamson **Address:** 2141 Rosecrans Ave. El Segundo, CA 90245 **Phone:** 310-726-7600 **Website:** http://www.unocal.com	**GANNETT** **CEO:** Douglas H. McCorkindale **Address:** 7950 Jones Branch Dr. McLean, VA 22107 **Phone:** 703-854-6000 **Website:** http://www.gannett.com	**GATEWAY** **CEO:** Theodore W. Waitt **Address:** 14303 Gateway Place Poway, CA 92064 **Phone:** 858-848-3401 **Website:** http://www.gateway.com	**SMITHFIELD FOODS** **CEO:** Joseph W. Luter III **Address:** 200 Commerce St. Smithfield, VA 23430 **Phone:** 757-365-3000 **Website:** http://www.smithfieldfoods.com
INTERPUBLIC **CEO:** John J. Dooner Jr. **Address:** 1271 Sixth Ave. New York, NY 10020 **Phone:** 212-399-8000 **Website:** http://www.interpublic.com	**SONIC AUTOMOTIVE** **CEO:** O. Bruton Smith **Address:** 5401 E. Independence Blvd. Charlotte, NC 28212 **Phone:** 704-566-2400 **Website:** http://www.sonicautomotive.com	**SAKS** **CEO:** R. Brad Martin **Address:** 750 Lakeshore Pkwy. Birmingham, AL 35211 **Phone:** 205-940-4000 **Website:** http://www.saksincorporated.com	**ROHM & HAAS** **CEO:** Rajiv L. Gupta **Address:** 100 Independence Mall W. Philadelphia, PA 19106 **Phone:** 215-592-3000 **Website:** http://www.rohmhaas.com
NAVISTAR INTERNATIONAL **CEO:** John R. Horne **Address:** 4201 Winfield Rd. Warrenville, IL 06555 **Phone:** 630-753-5000 **Website:** http://www.navistar.com	**CORNING** **CEO:** John W. Loose **Address:** 1 Riverfront Plaza Corning, NY 14831 **Phone:** 607-974-9000 **Website:** http://www.corning.com	**LENNAR** **CEO:** Stuart A. Miller **Address:** 700 N.W. 107th Ave. Miami, FL 33172 **Phone:** 305-559-4000 **Website:** http://www.lennar.com	**CONECTIV** **CEO:** Howard E. Cosgrove **Address:** 800 King St. Wilmington, DE 19899 **Phone:** 302-429-3018 **Website:** http://www.conectiv.com
CENTEX **CEO:** Laurence E. Hirsch **Address:** 2728 N. Harwood St. Dallas, TX 75201 **Phone:** 214-981-5000 **Website:** http://www.centex.com	**DEAN FOODS** **CEO:** Gregg L. Engles **Address:** 2515 McKinney Ave. Dallas, TX 75201 **Phone:** 214-303-3400 **Website:** http://www.deanfoods.com	**AVISTA** **CEO:** Gary G. Ely **Address:** 1411 E. Mission Ave. Spokane, WA 99202 **Phone:** 509-489-0500 **Website:** http://www.avistacorp.com	**SERVICE MASTER** **CEO:** Jonathan P. Ward **Address:** 2300 Warrenville Road Downers Grove, IL 60515 **Phone:** 630-271-1300 **Website:** http://www.svm.com

PPL **CEO:** William F. Hecht **Address:** 2 N. Ninth St. Allentown, PA 18101 **Phone:** 610-774-5151 **Website:** http://www.pplweb.com	**MEDTRONIC** **CEO:** Arthur D. Collins Jr. **Address:** 710 Medtronic Pkwy. Minneapolis, MN 55432 **Phone:** 763-514-4000 **Website:** http://www.medtronic.com	**FORTUNE BRANDS** **CEO:** Norman H. Wesley **Address:** 300 Tower Pkwy. Lincolnshire, IL 60069 **Phone:** 847-484-4400 **Website:** http://www.fortunebrands.com	**PRAXAIR** **CEO:** Dennis H. Reilley **Address:** 39 Old Ridgebury Rd. Danbury, CT 06810 **Phone:** 203-837-2000 **Website:** http://www.praxair.com
AIR PRODUCTS & CHEMICALS **CEO:** John P. Jones III **Address:** 7201 Hamilton Blvd. Allentown, PA 18195 **Phone:** 610-481-4911 **Website:** http://www.airproducts.com	**PROVIDIAN FINANCIAL** **CEO:** Joseph W. Saunders **Address:** 201 Mission St. San Francisco, CA 94105 **Phone:** 415-543-0404 **Website:** http://www.providian.com	**R.R. Donnelley & Sons** **CEO:** William L. Davis **Address:** 77 W. Wacker Dr. Chicago, IL 60601 **Phone:** 312-326-8000 **Website:** http://www.rrdonnelley.com	**AMERICAN FAMILY INS. GROUP** **CEO:** Harvey R. Pierce **Address:** 6000 American Pkwy. Madison, WI 53783 **Phone:** 608-249-2111 **Website:** http://www.amfam.com
CUMMINS **CEO:** Theodore M. Solso **Address:** 500 Jackson St. Columbus, IN 47201 **Phone:** 812-377-5000 **Website:** http://www.cummins.com	**VF** **CEO:** Mackey J. McDonald **Address:** 628 Green Valley Rd. Greensboro, NC 27408 **Phone:** 336-547-6000 **Website:** http://www.vfc.com	**USA NETWORKS** **CEO:** Barry Diller **Address:** 152 W. 57th St. New York, NY 10019 **Phone:** 212-314-7300 **Website:** http://www.usanetwork.com	**ENGELHARD** **CEO:** Barry W. Perry **Address:** 101 Wood Ave. Iselin, NJ 08830 **Phone:** 732-205-5000 **Website:** http://www.engelhard.com
IDACORP **CEO:** Jan B. Packwood **Address:** 1221 W. Idaho St. Boise, ID 83702 **Phone:** 208-388-2200 **Website:** http://www.idacorpinc.com	**FEDERAL-MOGUL** **CEO:** Frank E. Macher **Address:** 26555 Northwestern Hwy. Southfield, MI 48034 **Phone:** 248-354-7700 **Website:** http://WWW.federal-mogul.com	**CHARLES SCHWAB** **CEO:** Charles R. Schwab **Address:** 101 Montgomery St. San Francisco, CA 94104 **Phone:** 415-627-7000 **Website:** http://www.schwab.com	**SHERWIN-WILLIAMS** **CEO:** Christopher M. Connor **Address:** 101 Prospect Ave. N.W. Cleveland, OH 44115 **Phone:** 216-566-2000 **Website:** http://www.sherwin.com
STATE STREET CORP. **CEO:** David A. Spina **Address:** 225 Franklin St. Boston, MA 02110 **Phone:** 617-786-3000 **Website:** http://www.statestreet.com	**EASTMAN CHEMICALS** **CEO:** J. Brian Ferguson **Address:** One Eastman Rd. Kingsport, TN 37660 **Phone:** 423-229-2000 **Website:** http://www.eastman.com	**BJ s WHOLESALE CLUB** **CEO:** John J. Nugent **Address:** 1 Mercer Rd. Natick, MA 01760 **Phone:** 508-651-7400 **Website:** http://www.bjs.com	**GOODRICH** **CEO:** David L. Burner **Address:** 2730 West Tyvola Rd. Charlotte, NC 28217 **Phone:** 704-423-7000 **Website:** http://www.bfgoodrich.com
NORDSTROM **CEO:** Blake W. Nordstrom **Address:** 1617 Sixth Ave. Seattle, WA 98101 **Phone:** 206-628-2111 **Website:** http://www.nordstrom.com	**BAKER HUGHES** **CEO:** Michael E. Wiley **Address:** 3900 Essex Lane Houston, TX 77027 **Phone:** 713-439-8600 **Website:** http://www.bakerhughes.com	**IKON OFFICE SOLUTIONS** **CEO:** James J. Forese **Address:** 70 Valley Stream Pkwy. Malvern, PA 19355 **Phone:** 610-296-8000 **Website:** http://www.ikon.com	**RYDER SYSTEM** **CEO:** Gregory T. Swienton **Address:** 3600 N.W. 82nd Ave. Miami, FL 33166 **Phone:** 305-500-3726 **Website:** http://www.ryder.com
CAREMARK RX **CEO:** Edwin M. Crawford **Address:** 3000 Galleria Tower Birmingham, AL 35244 **Phone:** 205-733-8996 **Website:** http://www.caremarkrx.com	**PULTE HOMES** **CEO:** Mark J. O'Brien **Address:** 33 Bloomfield Hills Pkwy. Bloomfield Hills, MI 48304 **Phone:** 248-647-2750 **Website:** http://www.pulte.com	**TRIBUNE** **CEO:** John W. Madigan **Address:** 435 N. Michigan Ave. Chicago, IL 60611 **Phone:** 312-222-9100 **Website:** http://www.tribune.com	**Cnf** **CEO:** Gregory L. Quesnel **Address:** 3240 Hillview Ave. Palo Alto, CA 94304 **Phone:** 650-494-2900 **Website:** http://www.cnf.com
ALLIED WASTE INDUSTRIES **CEO:** Thomas H. Van Weelden **Address:** 15880 N. Greenway-Hayden Loop Scottsdale, AZ 85260 **Phone:** 480-627-2700 **Website:** http://www.alliedwaste.com	**APPLE COMPUTER** **CEO:** Steven P. Jobs **Address:** 1 Infinite Loop Cupertino, CA 95014 **Phone:** 408-996-1010 **Website:** http://www.apple.com	**TRANSMOTAIGNE** **CEO:** Donald H. Anderson **Address:** 370 17th St. Denver, CO 80202 **Phone:** 303-626-8200 **Website:** http://www.transmontaigne.com	**Barnes & Noble** **CEO:** Stephen Riggio **Address:** 122 Fifth Ave. New York, NY 10011 **Phone:** 212-633-3300 **Website:** http://www.barnesandnoble.com
SOUTHWEST AIRLINES **CEO:** James F. Parker **Address:** 2702 Love Field Dr. Dallas, TX 75235 **Phone:** 214-792-4000 **Website:** http://www.southwest.com	**DOLLAR GENERAL** **CEO:** Cal Turner Jr. **Address:** 100 Mission Ridge Goodlettsville, TN 37072 **Phone:** 615-855-4000 **Website:** http://www.dollargeneral.com	**TESORO PETROLEUM** **CEO:** Bruce A. Smith **Address:** 300 Concord Plaza Dr. San Antonio, TX 78216 **Phone:** 210-828-8484 **Website:** http://www.tesoropetroleum.com	**GRAYBAR ELECTRIC** **CEO:** Robert A. Reynolds Jr. **Address:** 34 N. Meramec Ave. St. Louis, MO 63105 **Phone:** 314-573-9200 **Website:** http://www.graybar.com

COUNTRY WIDE CREDIT INDUSTRIES **CEO:** Angelo R. Mozilo **Address:** 4500 Park Granada Calabasas, CA 91302 **Phone:** 818-225-3000 **Website:** http://www.countrywide.com B	**ITT INDUSTRIES** **CEO:** Louis J. Giuliano **Address:** 4 W. Red Oak Lane White Plains, NY 10604 **Phone:** 914-641-2000 **Website:** http://www.itt.com	**PINNACLE WEST CAPITAL** **CEO:** William J. Post **Address:** 400 N. Fifth St. Phoenix, AZ 85072 **Phone:** 602-250-1000 **Website:** http://www.pinnaclewest.com	**OXFORD HEALTH PLANS** **CEO:** Norman C. Payson M.D. **Address:** 48 Monroe Turnpike Trumbull, CT 06611 **Phone:** 203-459-6000 **Website:** http://www.oxfordhealth.com
AUTO ZONE **CEO:** Steve Odland **Address:** 123 S. Front St. Memphis, TN 38103 **Phone:** 901-495-6500 **Website:** http://www.autozone.com	**KB HOME** **CEO:** Bruce E. Karatz **Address:** 10990 Wilshire Blvd. Los Angeles, CA 90024 **Phone:** 310-231-4000 **Website:** http://www.kbhome.com	**DOVER** **CEO:** Thomas L. Reece **Address:** 280 Park Ave. New York, NY 10017 **Phone:** 212-922-1640 **Website:** http://www.dovercorporation.com	**CABLEVISION SYSTEMS** **CEO:** James L. Dolan **Address:** 1111 Stewart Ave. Bethpage, NY 11714 **Phone:** 516-803-2300 **Website:** http://www.cablevision.com
MATTEL **CEO:** Robert A. Eckert **Address:** 333 Continental Blvd. El Segundo, CA 90245 **Phone:** 310-252-2000 **Website:** http://www.mattel.com	**MCGRAW-HILL** **CEO:** Harold W. McGraw III **Address:** 1221 Sixth Ave. New York, NY 10020 **Phone:** 212-512-2000 **Website:** http://www.mcgraw-hill.com	**MICRON TECHNOLOGY** **CEO:** Steven R. Appleton **Address:** 8000 S. Federal Way Boise, ID 83707 **Phone:** 208-368-4000 **Website:** http://www.micron.com	**HEALTHSOUTH** **CEO:** Richard M. Scrushy **Address:** 1 HealthSouth Pkwy. Birmingham, AL 35243 **Phone:** 205-967-7116 **Website:** http://www.healthsouth.com
RADIOSHACK **CEO:** Leonard H. Roberts **Address:** 100 Throckmorton St. Fort Worth, TX 76102 **Phone:** 817-415-3700 **Website:** http://www.radioshackcorporation	**OFFICE MAX** **CEO:** Michael Feuer **Address:** 3605 Warrensville Ctr. Rd. Shaker Heights, OH 44122 **Phone:** 216-471-6900 **Website:** http://www.officemax.com	**AMEREN** **CEO:** Charles W. Mueller **Address:** 1901 Chouteau Ave. St. Louis, MO 63103 **Phone:** 314-621-3222 **Website:** http://www.ameren.com	**FOOT LOCKER** **CEO:** Matthew D. Serra **Address:** 112 W. 34th St New York, NY 10120 **Phone:** 212-720-3700 **Website:** http://www.footlocker-inc.com
OWENS CORNING **CEO:** David T. Brown **Address:** 1 Owens Corning Pkwy. Toledo, OH 43659 **Phone:** 419-248-8000 **Website:** http://www.owenscorning.com	**PARK PLACE ENTERTAINMENT** **CEO:** Thomas E. Gallagher **Address:** 3930 Howard Hughes Pkwy. Las Vegas, NV 89109 **Phone:** 702-699-5000 **Website:** http://www.parkplace.com	**MURPHY OIL** **CEO:** Claiborne P. Deming **Address:** 200 Peach St. El Dorado, AR 71730 **Phone:** 870-862-6411 **Website:** http://www.murphyoilcorp.com	**ADMINISTAFF** **CEO:** Paul J. Sarvadi **Address:** 19001 Crescent Springs Dr. Kingwood, TX 77339 **Phone:** 281-358-8986 **Website:** http://www.administaff.com
W.W. GRAINGER **CEO:** Richard L. Keyser **Address:** 100 Grainger Pkwy. Lake Forest, IL 60045 **Phone:** 847-535-1000 **Website:** http://www.grainger.com	**SIERRA PCIFIC RESOURCES** **CEO:** Walter M. Higgins III **Address:** 6100 Neil Road Reno, NV 89511 **Phone:** 775-834-4011 **Website:** http://www.sierrapacific.com	**D.R. HORTON** **CEO:** Donald J. Tomnitz **Address:** 1901 Ascension Blvd. Arlington, TX 76006 **Phone:** 817-856-8200 **Website:** http://www.drhorton.com	**BLACK & DECKER** **CEO:** Nolan D. Archibald **Address:** 701 E. Joppa Rd. Towson, MD 21286 **Phone:** 410-716-3900 **Website:** http://www.bdk.com
Adams Resources & Energy **CEO:** K.S. Adams Jr. **Address:** 4400 Post Oak Pkwy. Houston, TX 77027 **Phone:** 713-881-3600 **Website:** http://	**ESTEE LAUDER** **CEO:** Fred H. Langhammer **Address:** 767 Fifth Ave. New York, NY 10153 **Phone:** 212-572-4200 **Website:** http://www.elcompanies.com	**WILLIAMETTE INDUSTRIES** **CEO:** Steven R. Rogel **Address:** 1300 S.W. Fifth Avenue Portland, OR 97201 **Phone:** 503-227-5581 **Website:** http://www.weyerhaeuser.com	**JABIL CIRCUIT** **CEO:** Timothy L. Main **Address:** 10560 Ninth St. N. St. Petersburg, FL 33716 **Phone:** 727-577-9749 **Website:** http://www.jabil.com
PITNEY BOWES **Address:** 1 Elmcroft Rd. Stamford, CT 06926 **Phone:** 203-356-5000 **Website:** http://www.pitneybowes.com	**MAYTAG** **CEO:** Ralph F. Hake **Address:** 403 W. Fourth St. N. Newton, IA 50208 **Phone:** 641-792-7000 **Website:** http://www.maytagcorp.com	**QUANTUM** **CEO:** Michael A. Brown **Address:** 501 Sycamore Drive Milpitas, CA 95035 **Phone:** 408-894-4000 **Website:** http://www.quantum.com	**Mutual of Omaha Insurance** **CEO:** John W. Weekly **Address:** Mutual of Omaha Plaza Omaha, NE 68175 **Phone:** 402-342-7600 **Website:** http://www.mutualofomaha.com

DOLE FOOD CEO: David H. Murdock **Address:** 1 Dole Dr. Westlake Village, CA 91362 **Phone:** 818-874-4000 **Website:** http://www.dole.com	**HERSHEY FOODS** CEO: Rick H. Lenny **Address:** 100 Crystal A Dr. Hershey, PA 17033 **Phone:** 717-534-6799 **Website:** http://www.hersheys.com	**GOLDENWEST FINANCIAL** CEO: Herbert M. Sandler **Address:** 1901 Harrison St. Oakland, CA 94612 **Phone:** 510-446-3420 **Website:**	**ROCKWELL AUTOMATION** CEO: Don H. Davis Jr. **Address:** 777 E. Wisconsin Ave. Milwaukee, WI 53202 **Phone:** 414-212-5200 **Website:** http://www.rockwell.com
GOLDEN STATE BANCORP. CEO: Gerald J. Ford **Address:** 135 Main St. San Francisco, CA 94105 **Phone:** 415-904-1100 **Website:** http://www.goldenstate.com	**TEMPLE-INLAND** CEO: Kenneth M. Jastrow II **Address:** 1300 Mopac Expwy. South Austin, TX 78746 **Phone:** 512-434-8000 **Website:** http://www.temple-inland.com	**COX COMMUNICATIONS** CEO: James O. Robbins **Address:** 1400 Lake Hearn Dr. N.E. Atlanta, GA 30319 **Phone:** 404-843-5000 **Website:** http://www.cox.com	**PITTSTON** CEO: Michael T. Dan **Address:** 1801 Bayberry Ct. Richmond, VA 23226 **Phone:** 804-289-9600 **Website:** http://www.pittston.com
LONG DRUG STORES CEO: Harold R. Somerset **Address:** 141 N. Civic Dr. Walnut Creek, CA 94596 **Phone:** 925-937-1170 **Website:** http://www.longs.com	**LEXMARK INTERNATIONAL** CEO: Paul J. Curlander **Address:** 740 W. New Circle Rd. Lexington, KY 40550 **Phone:** 859-232-2000 **Website:** http://www.lexmark.com	**MELLON FINANCIAL CORP.** CEO: Martin G. McGuinn **Address:** 500 Grant St. Pittsburgh, PA 15258 **Phone:** 412-234-5000 **Website:** http://www.mellon.com	**PHELPS DODGE** CEO: J. Steven Whisler **Address:** 1 N. Central Ave. Phoenix, AZ 85004 **Phone:** 602-366-8100 **Website:** http://www.phelpsdodge.com
LEVI STRAUSS CEO: Philip A. Marineau **Address:** 1155 Battery St. San Francisco, CA 94111 **Phone:** 415-501-6000 **Website:** http://www.levistrauss.com	**NUCOR** CEO: Daniel R. DiMicco **Address:** 2100 Rexford Rd. Charlotte, NC 28211 **Phone:** 704-366-7000 **Website:** http://www.nucor.com	**SANMINA-SCI** CEO: Jure Sola **Address:** 2700 N. First St. San Jose, CA 95134 **Phone:** 408-964-3500 **Website:** http://www.sanmina.com	**ECHOSTAR COMMUNICATIONS** CEO: Charles W. Ergen **Address:** 5701 S. Santa Fe Littleton, CO 80120 **Phone:** 303-723-1000 **Website:** http://www.dishnetwork.com
KELLY SERVICES CEO: Terence E. Adderley **Address:** 999 W. Big Beaver Rd. Troy, MI 48084 **Phone:** 248-362-4444 **Website:** http://www.kellyservices.com	**HORMEL FOODS** CEO: Joel W. Johnson **Address:** 1 Hormel Place Austin, MN 55912 **Phone:** 507-437-5611 **Website:** http://www.hormel.com	**REGIONS FINANCIALS** CEO: Carl E. Jones Jr. **Address:** 417 N. 20th St. Birmingham, AL 35203 **Phone:** 205-944-1300 **Website:** http://www.regions.com	**GROUP 1 AUTOMOTIVE** CEO: B.B. Hollingsworth Jr. **Address:** 950 Echo Lane Houston, TX 77024 **Phone:** 713-647-5700 **Website:** http://www.group1auto.com
NORTHWESTERN CEO: Merle D. Lewis **Address:** 125 S. Dakota Ave. Sioux Falls, SD 57104 **Phone:** 605-978-2908 **Website:** http://www.northwestern.com	**SPX** CEO: John B. Blystone **Address:** 301 S. College St. Charlotte, NC 28202 **Phone:** 704-347-6800 **Website:** http://www.spx.com	**DARDEN RESTAURANTS** CEO: Joe R. Lee **Address:** 5900 Lake Ellenor Dr. Orlando, FL 32809 **Phone:** 407-245-4000 **Website:** http://www.darden.com	**AK STEEL HOLDINGS** CEO: Richard M. Wardrop Jr. **Address:** 703 Curtis St. Middletown, OH 45043 **Phone:** 513-425-5000 **Website:** http://www.aksteel.com
COOPER INDUSTRIES CEO: H. John Riley Jr. **Address:** 600 Travis St. Suite 5800Houston, TX 77002 **Phone:** 713-209-8400 **Website:** http://www.cooperindustries.com	**LEGGETT & PLATT** CEO: Felix E. Wright **Address:** 1 Leggett Rd. Carthage, MO 64836 **Phone:** 417-358-8131 **Website:** http://www.leggett.com	**PATHMARK STORES** CEO: James L. Donald **Address:** 200 Milik St. Carteret, NJ 07008 **Phone:** 732-499-3000 **Website:** http://www.pathmark.com	**AUTOLIV** CEO: Lars Westerberg **Address:** 3350 Airport Rd. Ogden, UT 84405 **Phone:** 801-625-9200 **Website:** http://www.autoliv.com
COMPUTER ASSOC. INTL. CEO: Sanjay Kumar **Address:** 1 Computer Associates Plaza Islandia, NY 11749 **Phone:** 631-342-5224 **Website:** http://www.ca.com	**NASH FINCH** CEO: Ron Marshall **Address:** 7600 France Ave. S. Edina, MN 55435 **Phone:** 952-832-0534 **Website:** http://www.nashfinch.com	**AMGEN** CEO: Kevin W. Sharer **Address:** 1 Amgen Center Dr. Thousand Oaks, CA 91320 **Phone:** 805-447-1000 **Website:** http://www.amgen.com	**MEADWESTVACO** CEO: John A. Luke Jr. **Address:** 1 High Ridge Park Stamford, CT 06905 **Phone:** 203-461-7400 **Website:** http://www.meadwestvaco.com
COMERICA CEO: Ralph W. Babb Jr. **Address:** 500 Woodward Ave. Detroit, MI 48226 **Phone:** 800-521-1190 **Website:** http://www.comerica.com	**JONES APPAREL GROUP** CEO: Sidney Kimmel **Address:** 250 Rittenhouse Circle Bristol, PA 19007 **Phone:** 215-785-4000 **Website:** http://www.jny.com	**MGM MIRAGE** CEO: L. Terrence Lanni **Address:** 3600 Las Vegas Blvd. S. Las Vegas, NV 89109 **Phone:** 702-693-7120 **Website:** http://www.mgmmirage.com	**ENCOMPASS SERVICES** CEO: Joseph M. Ivey Jr. **Address:** 3 Greenway Plaza Houston, TX 77046 **Phone:** 713-860-0100 **Website:** http://www.encompserv.com

STARWOOD HOTELS & RESORTS **CEO:** Barry S. Sternlicht **Address:** 777 Westchester Ave. White Plains, NY 10604 **Phone:** 914-640-8100 **Website:** http://www.starwood.com	**MAXTOR** **CEO:** Michael R. Cannon **Address:** 500 McCarthy Blvd Milpitas, CA 95035 **Phone:** 408-894-5000 **Website:** http://www.maxtor.com	Harrah's Entertainment **CEO:** Philip G. Satre **Address:** 1 Harrah's Court Las Vegas, NV 89119 **Phone:** 702-407-6000 **Website:** http://www.harrahs.com	**SPARTAN STORES** **CEO:** James B. Meyer **Address:** 850 76th St. S.W. Grand Rapids, MI 49518 **Phone:** 616-878-2000 **Website:** http://www.spartanstores.com
CDW COMPUTER CENTERS **CEO:** John A. Edwardson **Address:** 200 N. Milwaukee Ave. Vernon Hills, IL 60061 **Phone:** 847-465-6000 **Website:** http://www.cdw.com	**DANAHER** **CEO:** H. Lawrence Culp Jr. **Address:** 2099 Pennsylvania Ave. Washington, DC 20006 **Phone:** 202-828-0850 **Website:** http://www.danaher.com	**BALL** **CEO:** R. David Hoover **Address:** 10 Longs Peak Dr. Broomfield, CO 80021 **Phone:** 303-469-3131 **Website:** http://www.ball.com	**USA EDUCATION** **CEO:** Albert L. Lord **Address:** 11600 Sallie Mae Dr. Reston, VA 20193 **Phone:** 703-810-3000 **Website:** http://www.salliemae.com
JACOBS ENGINEERING GROUP **CEO:** Noel G. Watson **Address:** 1111 S. Arroyo Pkwy. Pasadena, CA 91105 **Phone:** 626-578-3500 **Website:** http://www.jacobs.com	**ENERGY EAST** **CEO:** Wesley W. von Schack **Address:** Albany, NY 12212 **Phone:** 518-434-3049 **Website:** http://www.energyeast.com	**BRUNSWICK** **CEO:** George W. Buckley **Address:** 1 N. Field Court Lake Forest, IL 60045 **Phone:** 847-735-4700 **Website:** http://www.brunswick.com	**INTERSTATE BAKERIES** **CEO:** Charles A. Sullivan **Address:** 12 E. Armour Blvd. Kansas City, MO 64111 **Phone:** 816-502-4000 **Website:** http://www.irin.com/ibc
LTV **CEO:** Glenn Moran **Address:** 200 Public Sq. Cleveland, OH 44114 **Phone:** 216-622-5000 **Website:** http://www.ltvsteel.com	**CEO:** J. Barclay Knapp **Address:** 110 East 59th St. New York, NY 10022 **Phone:** 212-906-8440 **Website:** http://www.ntl.com	**FAMILY DOLLAR STORES** **CEO:** Howard R. Levine **Address:** 10401 Old Monroe Rd. Matthews, NC 28105 **Phone:** 704-847-6961 **Website:** http://www.familydollar.com	**ROUNDY S** **CEO:** Gerald F. Lestina **Address:** 23000 Roundy Dr. Pewaukee, WI 53072 **Phone:** 262-953-7999 **Website:** http://www.roundys.com
CHARTER COMMUNICATIONS **CEO:** Carl E. Vogel **Address:** 12444 Powerscourt Dr. St.Louis, MO 63131 **Phone:** 314-965-0555 **Website:** http://www.chartercom.com	Becton Dickinson **CEO:** Edward J. Ludwig **Address:** 1 Becton Dr. Franklin Lakes, NJ 07417 **Phone:** 201-847-6800 **Website:** http://www.bd.com	**WESCO INTERNATIONAL** **CEO:** Roy W. Haley **Address:** 4 Station Square Pittsburgh, PA 15219 **Phone:** 412-454-2200 **Website:** http://www.wescodist.com	**SCANA** **CEO:** William B. Timmerman **Address:** 1426 Main St. Columbia, SC 29201 **Phone:** 803-217-9000 **Website:** http://www.scana.com
AMERICAN FINANCIAL GROUP **CEO:** Carl H. Lindner **Address:** One E. Fourth St. Cincinnati, OH 45202 **Phone:** 513-579-2121 **Website:** http://www.amfnl.com	**HOST MARRIOTT** **CEO:** Christopher J. Nassetta **Address:** 10400 Fernwood Rd. Bethesda, MD 20817 **Phone:** 301-380-9000 **Website:** http://www.hostmarriott.com	**AMES DEPARTMENT STORES** **CEO:** Joseph R. Ettore **Address:** 2418 Main St. Rocky Hill, CT 06067 **Phone:** 860-257-2000 **Website:** http://www.amesstores.com	**LIZ CALIBORNE** **CEO:** Paul R. Charron **Address:** 1441 Broadway New York, NY 10018 **Phone:** 212-354-4900 **Website:** http://www.lizclaiborne.com
YORK INTERNATIONAL **CEO:** Michael R. Young **Address:** 631 S. Richland Ave. York, PA 17403 **Phone:** 717-771-7890 **Website:** http://www.york.com	**FIRST AMERICAN CORP.** **CEO:** Parker S. Kennedy **Address:** 1 First American Way Santa Ana, CA 92707 **Phone:** 714-800-3000 **Website:** http://www.firstam.com	Kerr-McGee **CEO:** Luke R. Corbett **Address:** 123 Robert S. Kerr Ave. Oklahoma City, OK 73102 **Phone:** 405-270-1313 **Website:** http://www.Kerr-McGee.com	**MOHAWK INDUSTRIES** **CEO:** Jeffrey S. Lorberbaum **Address:** 160 S. Industrial Blvd. Calhoun, GA 30701 **Phone:** 706-629-7721 **Website:** http://www.mohawkind.com
WISCONSIN ENERGY **CEO:** Richard A. Abdoo **Address:** 231 W. Michigan St. Milwaukee, WI 53201 **Phone:** 414-221-2345 **Website:** http://www.wisenergy.com	**SOUTHTRUST CORP.** **CEO:** Wallace D. Malone Jr. **Address:** 420 N. 20th St. Birmingham, AL 35203 **Phone:** 205-254-5000 **Website:** http://www.southtrust.com	Quest Diagnostics **CEO:** Kenneth W. Freeman **Address:** 1 Malcolm Ave. Teterboro, NJ 07608 **Phone:** 201-393-5000 **Website:** http://www.questdiagnostics.com	**BIG LOTS** **CEO:** Michael J. Potter **Address:** 300 Phillipi Rd. Columbus, OH 43228 **Phone:** 614-278-6800 **Website:** http://www.biglots.com
CONSTELLATION ENERGY **CEO:** Mayo A Shattuck III **Address:** 250 W. Pratt St. Baltimore, MD 21201 **Phone:** 410-234-5000 **Website:** http://www.constellationenerg	**PACIFIC LIFE CORP.** **CEO:** Thomas C. Sutton **Address:** 700 Newport Center Dr. Newport Beach, CA 92660 **Phone:** 949-640-3011 **Website:** http://www.pacificlife.com	**SMITH INTERNATIONAL** **CEO:** Douglas R. Rock **Address:** 411 N. Sam Houston Pkwy. Ste 600Houston, TX 77060 **Phone:** 281-443-3370 **Website:** http://www.smith.com	**CORE-MARK INTERNATIONAL** **CEO:** Robert A. Allen **Address:** 395 Oyster Point Blvd. S. San Francisco, CA 94080 **Phone:** 650-589-9445 **Website:** http://www.coremark.com

EMCOR GROUP CEO: Frank T. MacInnis Address: 101 Merritt 7 Corporate Park Norwalk, CT 06851 Phone: 203-849-7800 Website: http://www.emcorgroup.com	**BETHLEHEM STEEL** CEO: Robert S. Miller Jr. Address: 1170 Eighth Ave. Bethlehem, PA 18016 Phone: 610-694-2424 Website: http://www.bethsteel.com	**JDS UNIPHASE** CEO: Jozef Straus PH.D. Address: 210 Baypointe Pkwy. San Jose, CA 95134 Phone: 408-434-1800 Website: http://www.jdsuniphase.com	**COOPER TIRE & RUBBER** CEO: Thomas A. Dattilo Address: 701 Lima Ave. Findlay, OH 45840 Phone: 419-423-1321 Website: http://www.coopertire.com
FOSTER WHEELER CEO: Raymond J. Milchovich Address: Perryville Corporate Park Clinton, NJ 08809 Phone: 908-730-4000 Website: http://www.fwc.com	**JEFFERSON PILOT** CEO: David A. Stonecipher Address: 100 N. Greene St. Greensboro, NC 27401 Phone: 336-691-3000 Website: http://www.jpfinancial.com	**LYONDELL CHEMICAL** CEO: Dan F. Smith Address: 1221 McKinney St. Houston, TX 77010 Phone: 713-652-7200 Website: http://www.lyondell.com	**COVENTRY HEALTHCARE** CEO: Allen F. Wise Address: 6705 Rockledge Dr. Bethesda, MD 20817 Phone: 301-581-0600 Website: http://www.coventryhealth.com
BORDERS GROUP CEO: Gregory P. Josefowicz Address: 100 Phoenix Dr. Ann Arbor, MI 48108 Phone: 734-477-1100 Website: http://www.bordersgroupinc.com	**BURLINGTON RESOURCES** CEO: Bobby S. Shackouls Address: 5051 Westheimer St. Houston, TX 77056 Phone: 713-624-9000 Website: http://www.br-inc.com	**AIRBORNE** CEO: Carl D. Donaway Address: 3101 Western Ave. Seattle, WA 98121 Phone: 206-830-4600 Website: http://www.airborne.com	**ANIXTER INTERNATIONAL** CEO: Robert W. Grubbs Jr. Address: 4711 Golf Rd. Skokie, IL 60076 Phone: 847-677-2600 Website: http://www.anixter.com
SHOPKO STORES CEO: William J. Podany Address: 700 Pilgrim Way Green Bay, WI 54304 Phone: 920-429-2211 Website: http://www.shopko.com	**ALLMERICA FINANCIAL** CEO: John F. O'Brien Address: 440 Lincoln St. Worcester, MA 01653 Phone: 508-855-1000 Website: http://www.allmerica.com	**COMDISCO** CEO: Norman P. Blake Jr. Address: 6111 N. River Rd. Rosemont, IL 60018 Phone: 847-698-3000 Website: http://www.comdisco.com	**UNION PLANTERS CORPORATION** CEO: Jackson W. Moore Address: 6200 Poplar Ave Memphis, TN 38119 Phone: 901-580-6000 Website: http://www.unionplanters.com
AMSOUTH BANCORP. CEO: C. Dowd Ritter Address: 1900 Fifth Ave. N. Birmingham, AL 35203 Phone: 205-320-7151 Website: http://www.amsouth.com	**USG** CEO: William C. Foote Address: 125 S. Franklin St. Chicago, IL 60606 Phone: 312-606-4000 Website: http://www.usg.com	**NSTART** CEO: Thomas J. May Address: 800 Boylston St. Boston, MA 02199 Phone: 617-424-2000 Website: http://www.nstaronline.com	**ARMSTRONG HOLDINGS** CEO: Michael D. Lockhart Address: 2500 Columbia Ave. Lancaster, PA 17603 Phone: 717-397-0611 Website: http://www.armstrong.com
PUGET ENERGY CEO: Stephen P. Reynolds Address: 411 108th Ave., NE Bellevue, WA 98004 Phone: 425-454-6363 Website: http://www.pse.com	**YELLOW** CEO: William D. Zollars Address: 10990 Roe Ave. Overland Park, KS 66211 Phone: 913-696-6100 Website: http://www.yellowcorp.com	**OGE ENERGY** CEO: Steven E. Moore Address: 321 N. Harvey Oklahoma City, OK 73102 Phone: 405-553-3000 Website: http://www.oge.com	**EQUITY OFFICE PROPERTIES** CEO: Timothy H. Callahan Address: 2 N. Riverside Plaza Chicago, IL 60606 Phone: 312-466-3300 Website: http://www.equityoffice.com
TENNECO AUTOMOTIVE CEO: Mark P. Frissora Address: 500 N. Field Drive Lake Forest, IL 60045 Phone: 847-482-5000 Website: http://www.tenneco-automotive.com	**NORTHERN TRUST CORPORATION** CEO: William A. Osborn Address: 50 S. LaSalle St. Chicago, IL 60675 Phone: 312-630-6000 Website: http://www.northerntrust.com	**STAFF LEASING** CEO: James F. Manning Address: 600 301 Blvd. W. Bradenton, FL 34205 Phone: 941-748-4540 Website: http://www.gevityhr.com	**AMAZON.COM** CEO: Jeffrey P. Bezos Address: 1200 12th Avenue S. Seattle, WA 98144 Phone: 206-266-2335 Website: http://www.amazon.com
HARLEY-DAVIDSON CEO: Jeffrey L. Bleustein Address: 3700 W. Juneau Ave. Milwaukee, WI 53208 Phone: 414-342-4680 Website: http://www.harley-davidson.com	**Aid Association for Lutherans** CEO: Bruce Nicholson Address: 4321 N. Ballard Rd. Appleton, WI 54919 Phone: 920-734-5721 Website: http://www.aal.org	**ENTERPRISE PRODUCTS** CEO: O.S. Andras Address: 2727 North Loop W. Houston, TX 77008 Phone: 713-880-6500 Website: http://www.epplp.com	**LENNOX INTERNATIONAL** CEO: Robert Schjerven Address: 2140 Lake Park Blvd. Richardson, TX 75080 Phone: 972-497-5000 Website: http://www.lennoxinternational	
WESTERN GAS RESOURCES CEO: Peter A Dea Address: 12200 N. Pecos St. Denver, CO 80234 Phone: 303-452-5603 Website: http://www.westerngas.com	**PERFORMANCE FOOD GROUP** CEO: C. Michael C. Gray Address: 12500 W. Creek Pkwy. Richmond, VA 23238 Phone: 804-484-7700 Website: http://www.pfgc.com	**PEPSIAMERICAS** CEO: Robert C. Pohlad Address: 60 S. Sixth St. Minneapolis, MN 55402 Phone: 612-661-3830 Website: http://www.pepsiamericas.com	**AMERICAN AXLE & MFG** CEO: Richard E. Dauch Address: 1840 Holbrook Ave. Detroit, MI 48212 Phone: 313-974-2000 Website: http://www.aam.com

C.H. Robinson Worldwide **CEO:** D. R. Verdoorn **Address:** 8100 Mitchell Rd. Suite 200Eden Prairie, MN 55344 **Phone:** 952-937-8500 **Website:** http://www.chrobinson.com	**CEO:** Edward L. Kuntz **Address:** 680 S. Fourth St. Louisville, KY 40202 **Phone:** 502-596-7300 **Website:** http://www.kindredhealthcare.	DEVON ENERGY **CEO:** J. Larry Nichols **Address:** 20 North Broadway Oklahoma City, OK 73102 **Phone:** 405-235-3611 **Website:** http://www.devonenergy.com	SEALED AIR **CEO:** William V. Hickey **Address:** Park 80 East Saddle Brook, NJ 07663 **Phone:** 201-791-7600 **Website:** http://www.sealedair.com
HILTON HOTELS **CEO:** Stephen F. Bollenbach **Address:** 9336 Civic Center Dr. Beverly Hills, CA 90210 **Phone:** 310-278-4321 **Website:** http://www.hilton.com	NEW YORK TIMES **CEO:** Russell T. Lewis **Address:** 229 W. 43rd St. New York, NY 10036 **Phone:** 212-556-1234 **Website:** http://www.nytco.com		

Appendix B

Instrument

Executive Coaching at the CEO Level

How would you rate your own understanding of Executive Coaching?
1- Very good   2- Adequate   3- Poor   4- Not sure

Executive Coaching is different from Consulting.
1- True   2- False   3- Not sure

Based on what you know or have heard, Executive Coaching as a paid-for service, like Consulting, will make the quality of CEOs
1- Much better   2- Somewhat better   3- Somewhat worse
4- Much worse   5- Not Sure

Do you agree or disagree with CEOs hiring coaches?
1-Strongly agree   2-Agree   3-disagree
4-Strongly disagree   5-Not sure

Have you ever hired a coach?
1-Yes   2-No

If you answered with NO , would you be very willing, somewhat willing, not very willing, or not at all willing to hire an Executive Coach?
1-Very willing   2-Somewhat willing
3-Not very willing   4-Not at all willing

If you re hiring an executive coach, you would prefer an:
1-Internal coach (within the company)
2-External coach (outsider)
3-Not necessary

When hiring a coach, you would look for one through:
1-Human resources   2-The Net
3-Friend   4-Outside consultant

On average, CEOs don't like the public to know about their executive coaching relationship.
1-True   2-False   3-Not sure

It s better for CEOs, going under coaching, to have their coaching sessions conducted:
1-In person - on site   2-In person - away from company premises
3-Over the telephone   4-Doesn t matter

Coaching should be limited to:
1-New CEOs   2-Experienced CEOs
3-Both   4-Management below CEO level
5-Unlimited

Research and Support for Executive Coaching should:
1-Continue   2-Stop   3-Not sure

Appendix C

Authorizations to Modify Instrument, and to Quote/Use Literature Material

From: William Hallman [hallman@rci.rutgers.edu]
Sent: Monday, June 10, 2002 1:55 PM
To: Fanasheh, Husam A
Subject: RE:

Fine if you want to use the instrument. Would be please if you sent me a copy of your modifications and a brief description of your results when you have completed your study.

William K. Hallman, PhD.
Associate Director
Food Biotechnology Program
Food Policy Institute (FPI)
Rutgers University
ASB III, 3 Rutgers Plaza
New Brunswick, NJ 08901
Phone: 732.932.1966 x3103
Fax: 732.932.9544

-----Original Message-----
From: Fanasheh, Husam A [mailto:husam.a.fanasheh@boeing.com]
Sent: Monday, June 10, 2002 11:21 AM
To: 'hallman@aesop.rutgers.edu'
Subject:

Dear Dr. William Hallman,
Around 8 months ago, I got a permission from you to use the instrument you used in collecting opinions about using biochemical on the East Coast. However, I just can't find it. And for the requirements, I need your permission again to use the instrument (after modifying it), to measure the perception of executive coaching among the Fortune 500 CEOs.
Thank you for your time.

Sam Fanasheh
Pepperdine University.

To: Fanasheh, Husam A
Subject: FW: A Pepperdine University Doctoral Study

Hello Sam

Thank you for your enquiry. My report which you found details of on the IES website includes an extensive bibliography of the sources which I used for my literature review. You may therefore wish to purchase a copy of the report. The only other research on executive coaching which I would advise as essential reading is:

Hall DT, Otazo KL and hollenbeck GP, 'Behind closed doors: What really happens in Executive Coaching?', Organisational Dynamics, Winter 1999.

My research approach was qualitative, utilising in depth interviews with executive coaches and commissioners and a Forum of commissioners. I did not conduct a survey on this occassion. Actually the Hall et al study was also qualitative, utilising interviews with executive coaches and executives being coached. You may quote and use contents of the report as necessary. It is definately time for an independent survey of executive coaching, so I wish you well, and very much look forward to seeing your results published in due course.

Alison

> ---
> ------------------
> Alison Carter
> Principal Research Fellow
> T: 01273 873673
> F: 01273 690430
> E: alison.carter@employment-studies.co.uk
>
> Institute for Employment Studies
> Registered Office:
> Mantell Building, University of Sussex, Brighton BN1 9RF, UK
> Registered in England no. 931547
> IES is a charitable company limited by guarantee.
> Registered charity no. 258390
> http://www.employment-studies.co.uk

Appendix D

Survey Cover Letter

TO: **Mr. Joe Doe, Chief Executive Officer**
                         The XYZ Company
                         1303 Street Way
                         City, CA 92647

FROM: **H. Fanasheh, Doctoral Candidate**
                         Pepperdine University
                         Culver City, CA 90807

RE: **Executive Coaching Research**

DATE: **August 02, 2002**

Dear Mr. Doe,

I am a doctoral student examining the *perception* of *executive coaching* among the top 500 CEOs in the U.S. . As one of the targeted population, I am very interested in your thoughts and opinions of executive coaching.

Your input helps shape the direction of the executive coaching services that benefit executives and organizations.

The survey should take no more than 3.5 minutes to complete. To thank you for completing the survey, we will provide you with a copy of the findings.

Please take part in this research. And for your convenience, a postage-paid, pre-addressed envelope is enclosed.

Your individual responses will be held in strictest confidence with results provided only in combination with the responses of others.

Thank you very much for your time.

Sincerely,

Husam Fanasheh
Doctoral Student
Pepperdine University

Printed in the United States
205015BV00003B/8/A